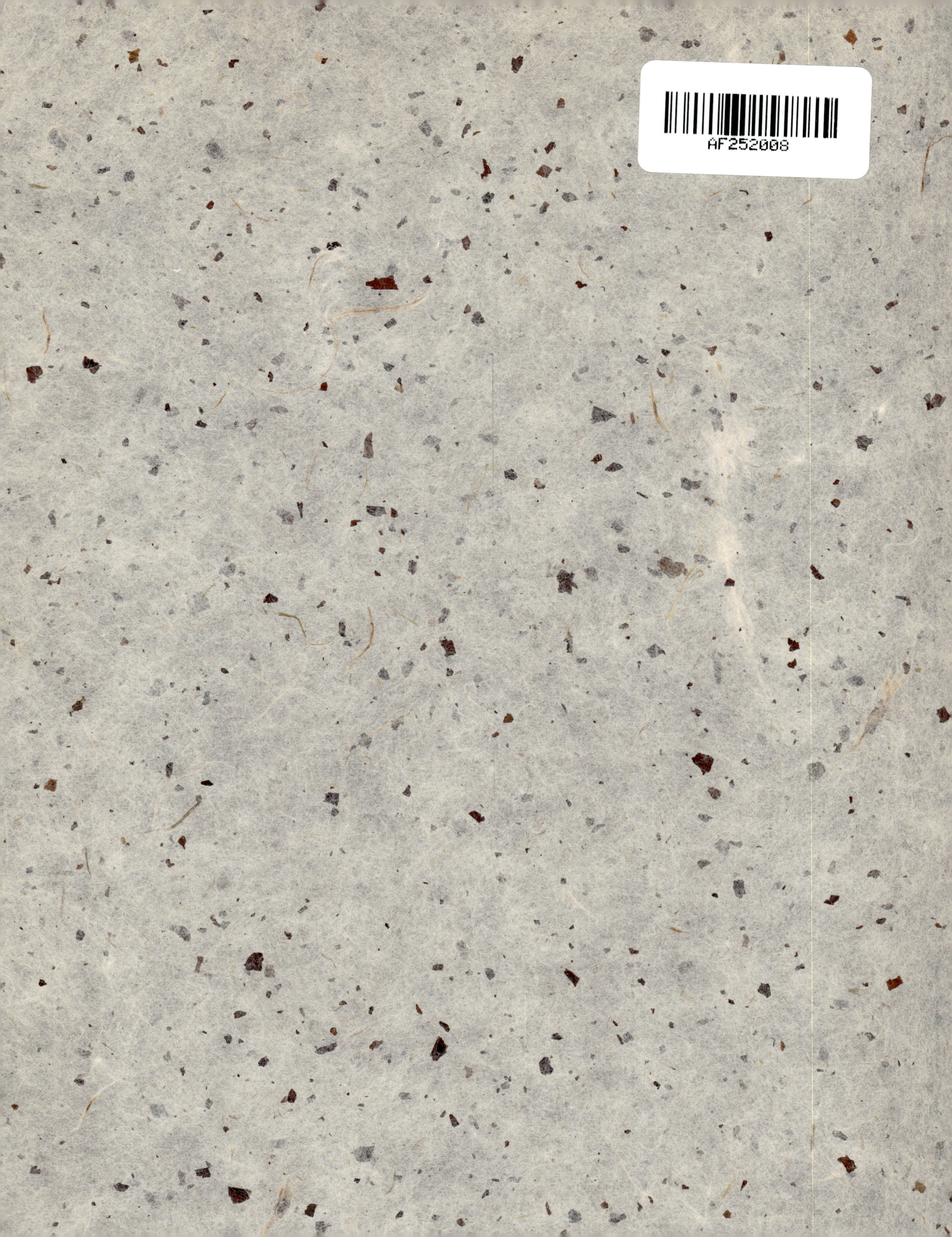

Essays by Frances Colpitt and Kerry Brougher

The Museum of Contemporary Art, Los Angeles

M A R K *L E R E*

New and Selected Work

This catalogue is published on the occasion of a two-part exhibition of the work of Mark Lere.

HALO/WHEEL July 21 – October 15, 1984

MARK LERE *New and Selected Work* February 13 – May 26, 1985

Editor: Julia Brown

Editorial assistants: Kerry Brougher and Connie Butler

Copyright © 1985 by The Museum of Contemporary Art, Los Angeles

Library of Congress Catalogue Card Number: 84-043091   ISBN:0-914357-08-5

Design: Haycock Kienberger, Los Angeles
Typesetting: Women's Graphic Center
Printing: Castle Press, Pasadena

ACKNOWLEDGEMENTS

Richard Koshalek *Director*

Any exhibition depends on the support and encouragement of many individuals and this two-part exhibition of the work of Mark Lere allows the Museum to extend thanks and credit to a number of people outside the art community in much the same way *Halo/Wheel* extended the parameters of the Museum beyond the walls of The Temporary Contemporary.

¶ We are most grateful to Mark Lere for his collaboration in the realization of this exhibition and its catalogue and for the assistance that he and Debra Burchett provided at every step along the way.

¶ *Halo/Wheel* would not have been possible without the invaluable cooperation of many departments of the City of Los Angeles and the City Council. In particular, we would like to thank Fred Croton, General Manager, Department of Cultural Affairs; Maureen Kindel, President of the Board of Public Works; David Reed, Assistant Director of the Department of Public Works; Norman R. Giard, Chief Inspector of the Street Use Inspection Division; Guy Quinn, Principal Transportation Engineer, Department of Transportation; Joel Breitbart, Assistant General Manager, Planning and Development, Department of Recreation and Parks; Alonzo Carmichael, Planning Officer, Department of Recreation and Parks; Ted Heyl, Assistant Planning Officer, Department of Recreation and Parks; Camille Didier, Administrative Assistant, Department of Recreation and Parks; Eugene Gagne, Supervising Civil Engineer, Los Angeles County Flood Control District; and Thomas Falk, Engineering Evaluation Section, the Army Corps of Engineers. We would also like to thank Al Nodal, Director of the Otis/Parsons Gallery, who cooperated in every way in realizing the part of *Halo/Wheel* for MacArthur Park.

¶ We thank Frances Colpitt and Kerry Brougher for their perceptive essays providing insight into the work of Mark Lere, and Laurie Haycock and Tom Kienberger of Haycock Kienberger for their design of this catalogue and the map for *Halo/Wheel*. Dennis Keeley, Doug Parker, John Eden, and Squidds and Nunns provided the excellent photographs.

¶ Julia Brown, Senior Curator, was curator for both *Halo/Wheel* and *Mark Lere, New and Selected Work* and served as editor of this catalogue. Kerry Brougher, Assistant Curator, organized many facets of both exhibitions and the catalogue, and was responsible for coordination with City departments for *Halo/ Wheel*. Sherri Geldin, Administrator, played an essential role in realizing this project overall. Connie Butler, Curatorial Intern, and Patricia Paine and June Kino-Cullen, Curatorial Secretaries, provided conscientious assistance, as did volunteers Maria Dion, Pepper Eisner, and Ellen Kwan. Kim Bradley, Registrar, arranged the transportation of the work and John Bowsher, Operations Manager, coordinated all aspects of the installation for both exhibitions. Special thanks is given to Marc O'Carroll, David French, and the entire installation crew for their skills in fabricating and installing the many elements of *Halo/Wheel*.

¶ We thank our full Board of Trustees and its Program Committee for their ongoing support of the Museum's exhibition programs. This exhibition is one of the Museum's *In Context* series in which new work is commissioned from American artists and is placed in the context of previous work and in an environment appropriate to the artist's work.

¶ The Museum expresses its gratitude to Toby Franklin K. Wilcox of Keeline-Wilcox Nurseries for the donation of the cypress trees that were integral to the Elysian Park site of *Halo/Wheel*. *Halo/Wheel* was funded in part by the Los Angeles Olympic Organizing Committee and was an Olympic Arts Festival exhibition, Times-Mirror official festival sponsor.

INTRODUCTION

Julia Brown *Senior Curator*

4

As part of its commitment to the support, exhibition and documentation of the work of individual artists, The Museum of Contemporary Art has organized this exhibition and catalogue of the recent work of Los Angeles artist Mark Lere. In recognition of Lere's involvement with sited sculpture and his exploration of concepts of fragmentary, multi-element works, the first part of this exhibition, a single public work titled *Halo/Wheel*, took place in twelve locations around the city of Los Angeles. The second part of this exhibition, within museum walls, *Mark Lere, New and Selected Work*, surveys recent work in a concentrated space with new pieces commissioned by the Museum.

¶ Lere makes enigmatic objects from industrial materials evoking images of urban mechanical processes as well as organic and natural forces. Lere's use of geometry is combined with a handmade rough quality retained in his materials, resulting in static objects that contain a sense of mystery, impending movement and contained force. His objects are made with an understanding both of their surroundings (in placement and in relationship one to another) and of being part of something larger (the suggestion of what the object has been cut out of or what has been removed to make the object). Lere's sculpture and drawings evoke the potency of built structures and spaces using images of architecture, the body and nature.

¶ The second part of the exhibition brings together selected recent work with works made specifically for the exhibition spaces and architecture of The Temporary Contemporary. Though each work stands on its own, the installation, designed by the artist, is intended as a dialogue among objects, within gestures and with the space itself.

¶ It is a pleasure to introduce the catalogue for this two-part exhibition, organized and designed in concert with the artist.

MARK LERE

Frances Colpitt

5

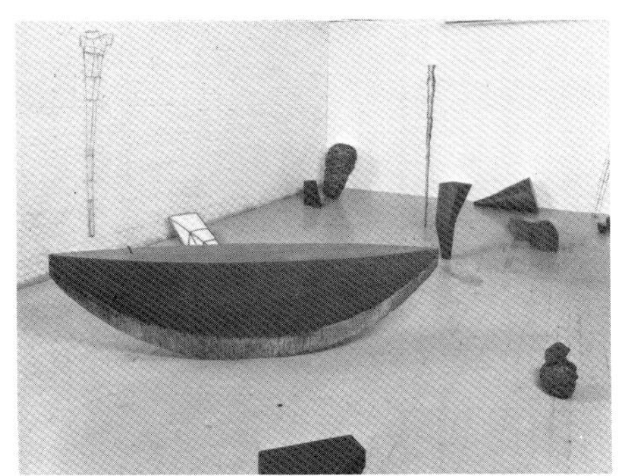

1 Sympathetic Structures, 1984
Mixed media studio installation

The true power of sculpture lies in its physicality, its literal spatial existence. Sculpture stimulates through kinesthetic provocation or identification in which the viewer's body responds, in any number of ways, to the "occupied zone" of the gallery or landscape. Great sculpture, however, involves more than physicality. What holds a single piece or an installation together—beyond formal cohesion or aesthetic unity—is a coherent conceptual envelope or skeleton called meaning and content. Mark Lere's sculpture defies the restraints of purely formal abstraction and simple space consumption. The ambience an installation of his work provides is at once intellectual and poetic, enhanced by the sculpture's physical and objective qualities.

¶ In 1978, Lere began a series of sculptures based on the concept of the stage. Prior to the "stages," his work was basically experimental, exploring various media, styles, materials and tech-

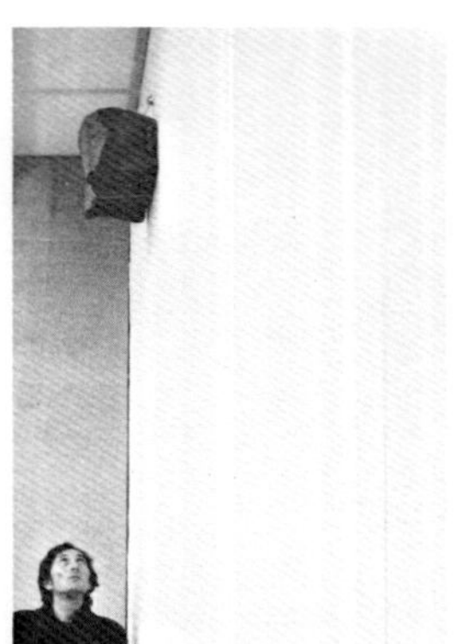

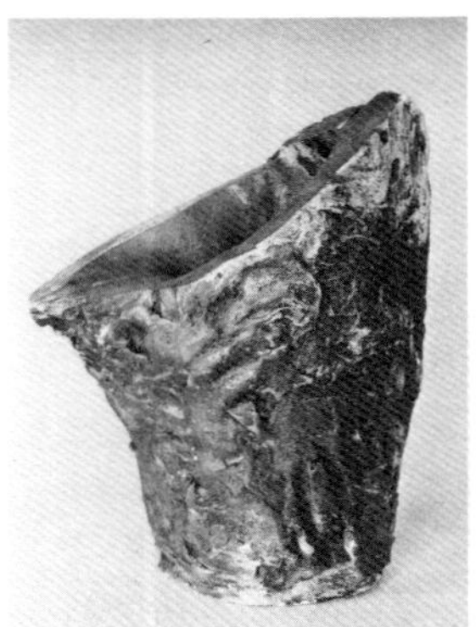

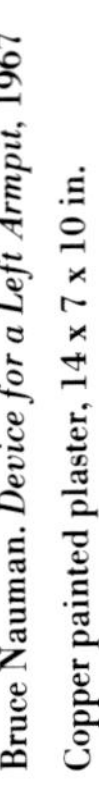

niques. Of significant influence on his development was the generation of artists reacting to the tenets of Minimalism. He cites those connected to *Arte Povera*, and Giovanni Anselmo in particular. Their emphasis on non-traditional, inelegant materials and the predominant role of nature is echoed in Lere's sculpture. Of interest as well were Dennis Oppenheim and Hans Haacke, whose broad explorations of natural and conventional systems must have struck a note of identification in the young sculptor. Like many artists in Los Angeles, Lere also benefited from and was inspired by the great mind and presence of Bruce Nauman. There are overt formal similarities in their work, especially in the hand-made, eccentric quality of the objects. When asked about influences, Lere persistently acknowledges Barry Le Va. The spread and scatter of material and the effect of an apparent random-ness are particularly evident in Lere's

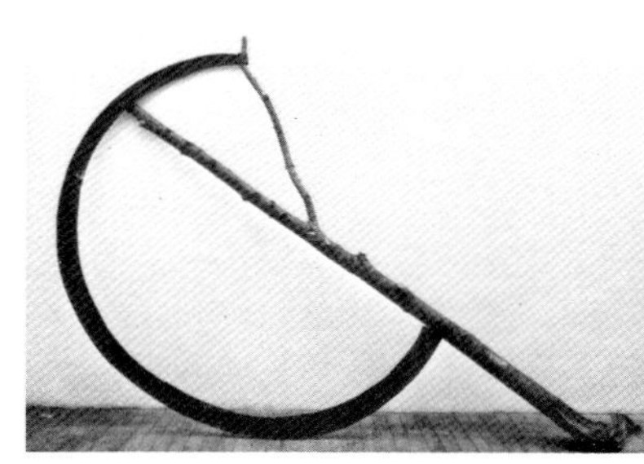

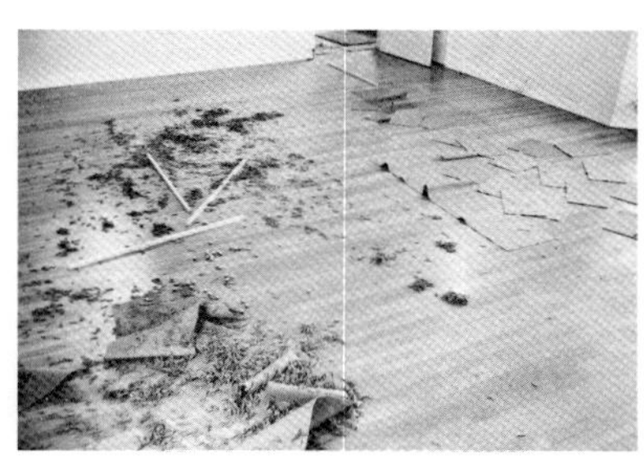

2 Drawing for *Water Suites: Stage*, 1981
Graphite and pencil on Herculene, 36 x 64 in.

C Giuseppe Penone. *Double Vegetal Gesture/Axe*, 1982
Wood, metal and cast bronze, 288 x 410 x 25 cm.

D Barry Le Va. *Two Continuous and Related Activities;*
Discontinued by the Act of Placing, 1967.
Ball bearings, felt and wood, dimensions variable

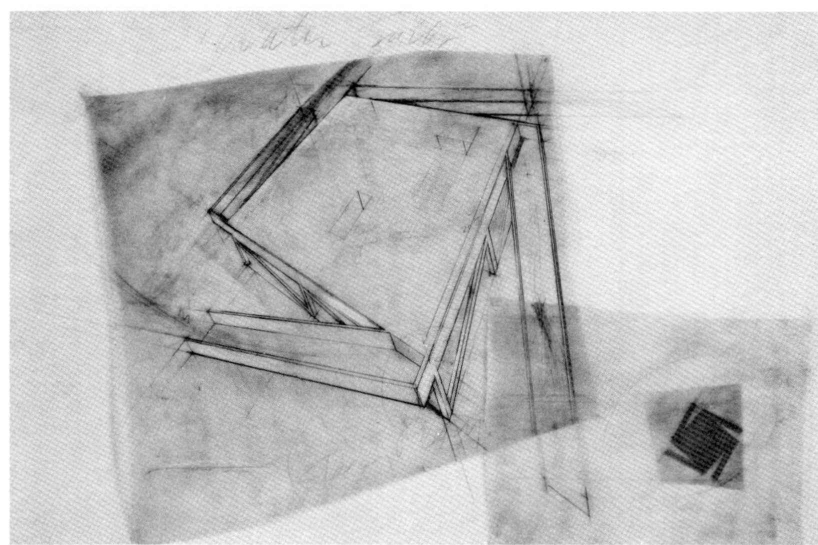

recent work. Although Le Va's work is process-oriented and completely non-objective, the two artists share an approach to conceptualist strategy and installation. What distinguishes all of this work from Minimal Art is the quality of being non-focused, with the field replacing the "specific object."[1] At the same time, Lere shares with many contemporary sculptors such as Joel Shapiro, Judy Pfaff and Tony Cragg, an involvement with suggestive imagery.

¶ Before he was able to devote all his time to making sculpture, Lere worked as a carpenter. His sculpture is characterized by the straightforward use of materials and construction techniques. He consistently chooses non-illusionistic, identifiable materials; instead of stone, bronze and marble, one finds industrial and building materials such as concrete, steel and plaster. Though finely crafted, the objects have a rough, flat-footed quality that specifically reacts against the polished slickness and anonymity of "fetish finish" art in Los Angeles.

¶ Lere's interpretations of his own work stress the quality of metaphor, an attitude justified by the abstract nature of the sculpture. It is clearly *not* non-representational work, and yet the objects parodied are not themselves the source of metaphor. In the *Fountains*, for example, what are at stake are traditional and historical associations connected with water-circulating monuments. Relevant to the *Crucibles* are all connotations—from alchemy to sculpture-making—of vessels used for melting metal. Lere's work is distinguished by its avoidance of specificity and literalness and its emphasis on allusion and connotation.

¶ Like many contemporary artists, Lere is interested in both intellectual and natural references and relationships. Implicated are sign, symbol, metaphor and illusion. Yet his work

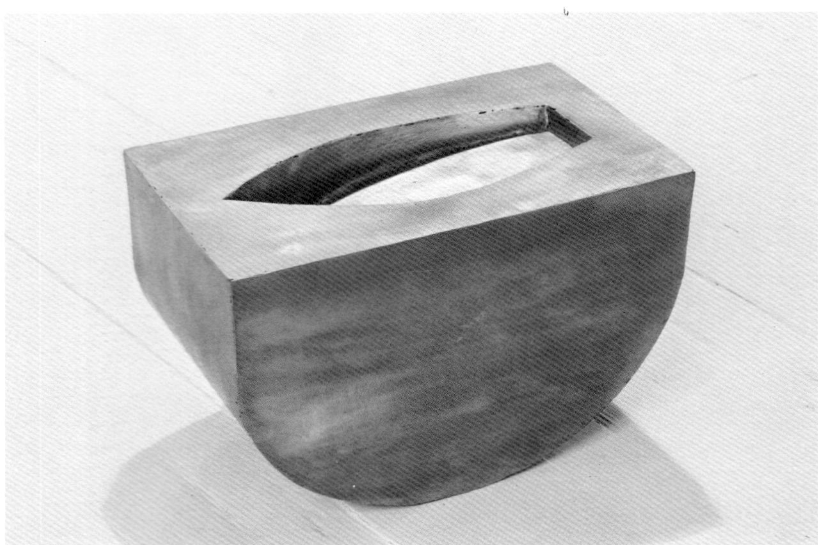

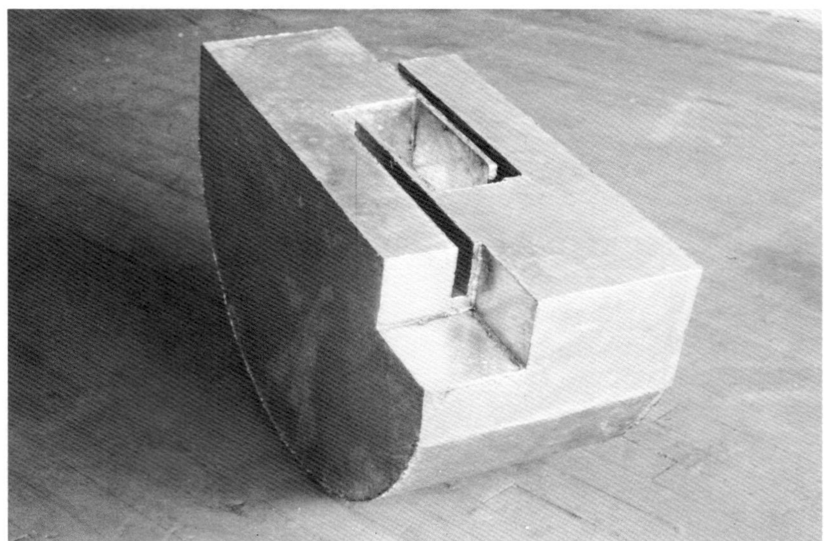

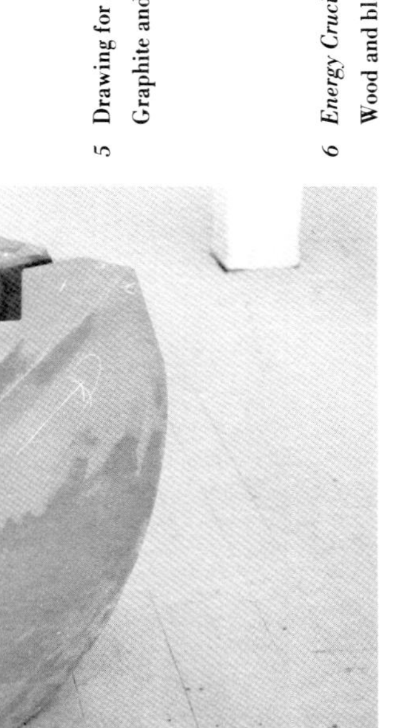

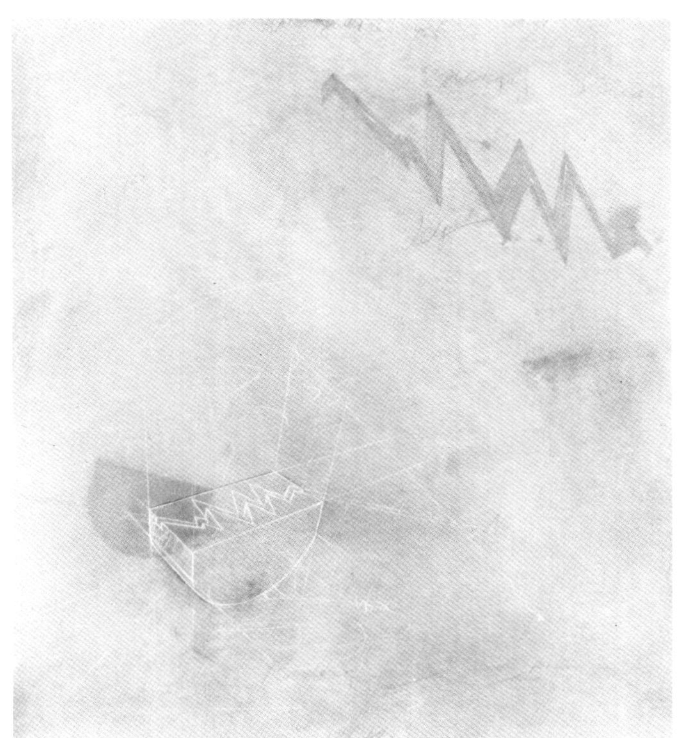

5 Drawing for *Energy Crucible*, 1981
Graphite and pencil on Herculene, 42 x 36 in.

6 *Energy Crucible*, 1981
Wood and blackboard paint, 24 x 36 x 16 in.

remains obstinately non-narrative, neither literary nor anecdotal. Literature and, by extension, narrative art are temporal and generally linear. In Lere's work, there is no specific sequence of events (or objects). Instead, the situations presented are cyclical or circular in that, as the artist has said, "Each new work alters the meaning of the previous one."[2] Because his work is referential, critics have concentrated on deciphering the imagery, as if it constituted the meaning of the sculpture. However, it is essential to go beyond a mere decoding of imagery to the work's substance and the powerful experiences it provokes.

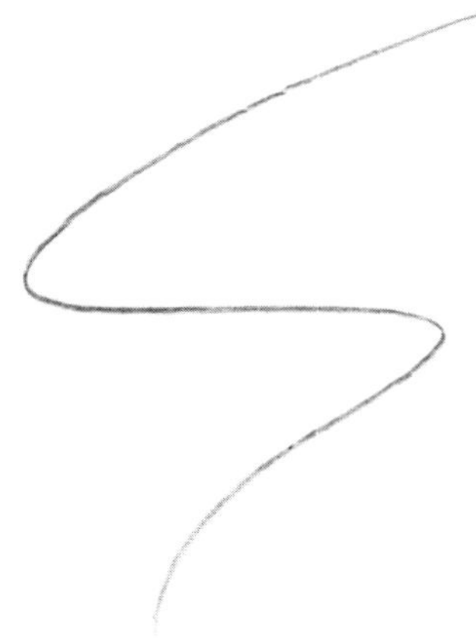

Two fairly distinct phases constitute Lere's work to date. The first, from the "Vertical Stages" to *Apsides House*, involved theatricality and the processes and imagery of architecture. Around 1980, Lere began a series of discrete, self-sufficient sculptures, which when juxtaposed carry on a meaningful dialogue with one another. Lere's earlier commitment had been less to object-making than to creating and manipulating space. The "stages" provide a kind of conflation of art and life, of the artificial and the mundane. This is best and quite literally illustrated by the "Room Stages," which reproduce individual rooms in Lere's small apartment. By elevating and spotlighting each construction, a psychologically familiar yet prohibitive space is created. This is what the artist calls a "metaphorical space," provoking the imagination by dramatizing the everyday.

¶ The "Room Stages" derive from the

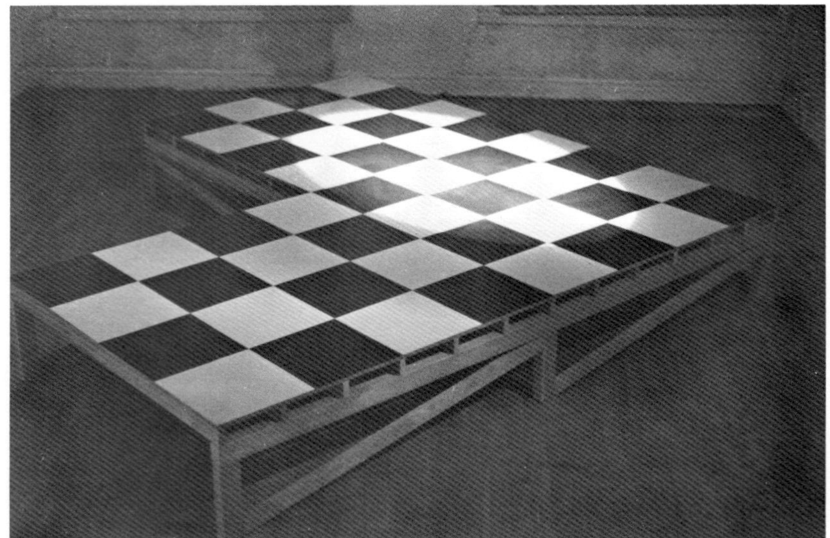

7 *Room Stage: Kitchen*, 1979
Wood, tile and lights, 12 x 144 x 144 in.

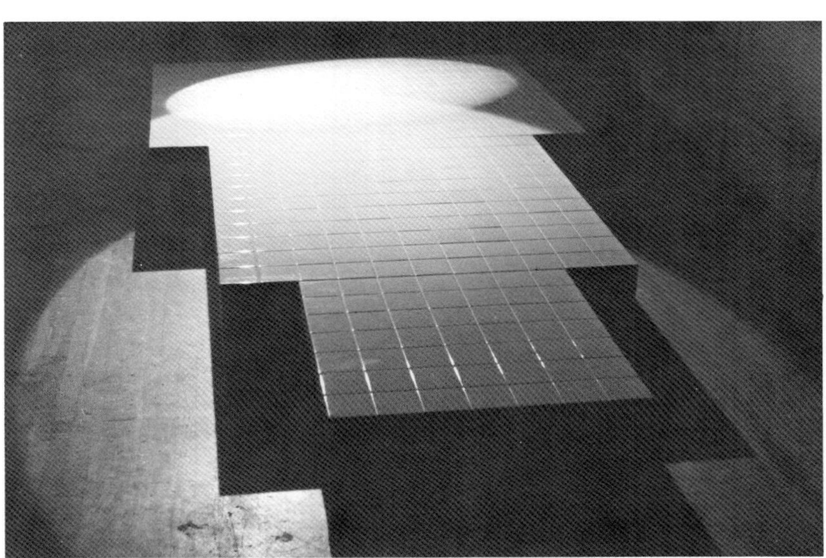

8 *New York Bathroom Stage*, 1978
Tiles and wood, 12 x 96 x 48 in.

artist's own environment, but they speak in a public voice about the impact and influences of architectural spaces on behavior. This very specific kind of control and orientation of the spectator requires one's imaginative participation. Lere's work needs an audience and is made for that audience. This attitude is at once generous and coersive, much like Bruce Nauman's: —————————————

I began to think about how you relate to a particular place . . . and then I began thinking about how to present this without making a performance, so that somebody else would have the same experience instead of just having to watch me have that experience . . . .
¶ I don't like the idea of free manipulation, of putting a bunch of stuff out there and letting people do what they want with it. I really had more specific kinds of experience in mind, and without having to write out a list of what people should do, I wanted to make play experiences unavailable just by the preciseness of the area.[3]

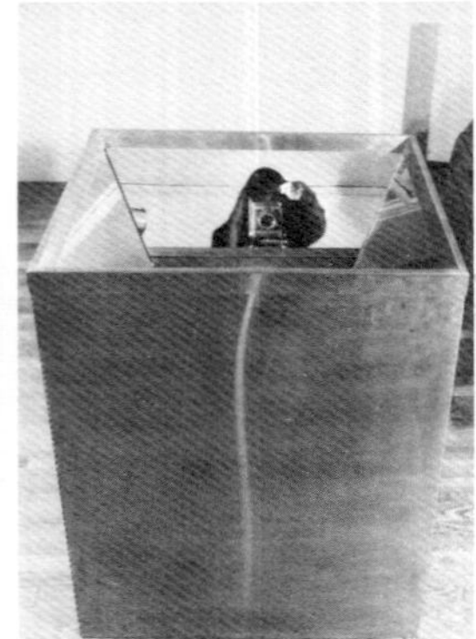

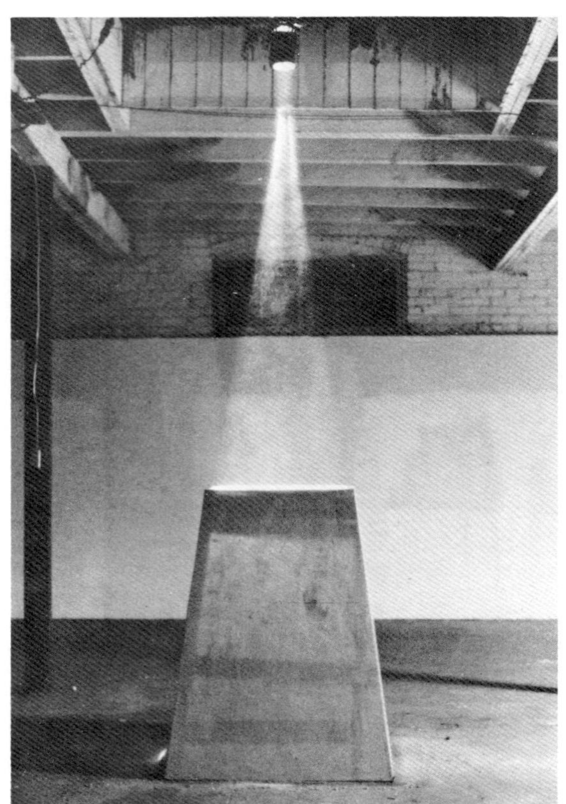

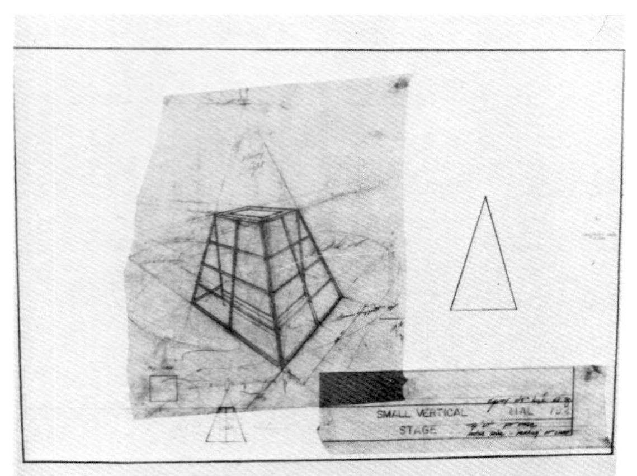

E   Robert Smithson. *Four-Sided Vortex*, 1965
Stainless steel and mirror, 35 x 28 x 28 in.

9   *Vertical Stage*, 1979
Light, wood and paint, 144 x 36 x 36 in.

10 Drawing for *Vertical Stage*, 1979
Blueprint, 24 x 36 in.

The earliest of Lere's "stages" directly and literally reorient the viewer. The "Vertical Stages" must be peered into from above (an unusual way to look at sculpture) to experience, in one case, a stepped series of shadows on the interior. This finds a parallel in Robert Smithson's *Four-Sided Vortex*, in which the mirrored interior well reflects the viewer as he bends his head over to see the work. The kind of directional orientation most of Lere's stages involve is, however, specifically architectural.

¶ Both sculpture and architecture require, from artist and viewer, a sense of place. They strive to stimulate an awareness of space through actual manipulation of material and form. The recent phenomenon of architectural sculpture, which includes the work of artists such as Alice Aycock, Mary Miss and Siah Armajani, has been well documented. This "fearless synthesizing," as Lucy Lippard has pointed

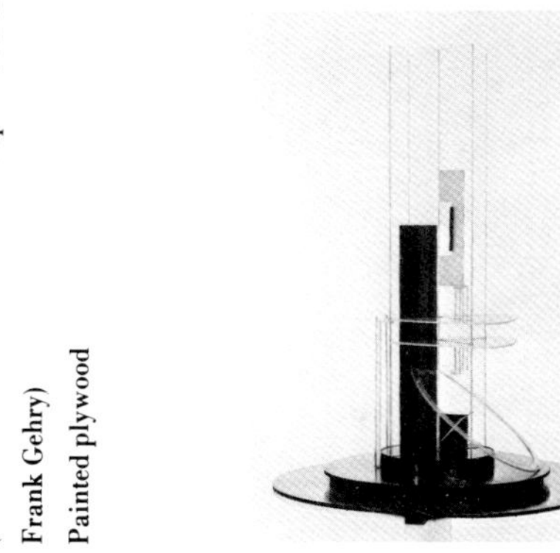

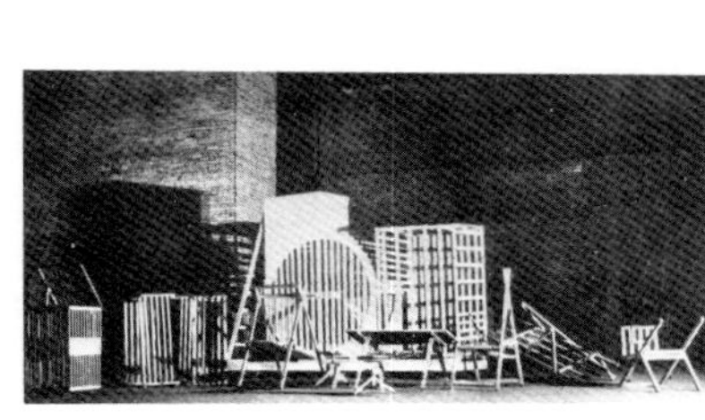

out, "has come to mean anything that imitates, simulates or suggests architecture's scale *or* its spatial effects *or* its images *or* its materials *or* its shelter functions."[4] What distinguishes architectural sculpture from *architecture* and establishes it as *sculpture* is its impracticality. Habitation may be implied and even possible, but it is not really the issue.

¶ As a precedent for architectural sculpture, Russian Constructivism of the 1920s was also motivated by more than pragmatic concerns. Although the function of Naum Gabo's *Column* of 1923 was never specified, it was designed with social and utilitarian implications. According to Christina Lodder, *Column* is, however, primarily an aesthetic object.[5] Its resemblance to Lere's *Apsides House* suggests that the Constructivists, like artists of the seventies, were interested in the possibilities of materials and the organization and articulation of space in an architectural context. This is perhaps less true for Tatlin's proposed *Monument to the Third International* and Gustav Klutsis's propaganda kiosks, although structural similarities are apparent in all such work. Perhaps closest of all ideologically to Mark Lere's large constructions are the theatrical set designs of Varvara Stepanova and Lyubov Popova, in which mechanical, architectural environments allude to a new order and culture.

¶ Lere's early work remains firmly within this Constructivist architectural mode but is distinguished by its conceptual, anti-functional nature. The simplest and most beautiful sculptures from this period are the "Door Swings." These small, elevated wooden platforms transcribe the arc of a door as it swings open or closed. Richard Artschwager's comments of 1967 entitled "The Hydraulic Doorcheck," perfectly illustrate the significance of Lere's "Door Swings." ——————— The irregular geometric shapes of the "Door Swings," like the "Room Stages," stress an aspect of our being-in-space. They render material what is only spatial by relying on a system of reversals, i.e., from negative to positive and functional to non-functional. The theatrical notions of presentation and artifice underlie all of Lere's architectural constructions. These are stages, flats and props, twice removed from functional architecture and once

The most striking property of doors (although not unique to doors) is resonance between two states, which can be conveniently labeled as "open" and "closed." Resonance is never a simple, unqualified fluctuation between two states; even so in this case. A door—at any given moment—is in a state of being closed with the possibility of its being opened, or in a state of being opened with the possibility of its being closed. This is not a speculative model for a door but a description of the state of affairs which immediately existed when the first door was brought into being.[6]

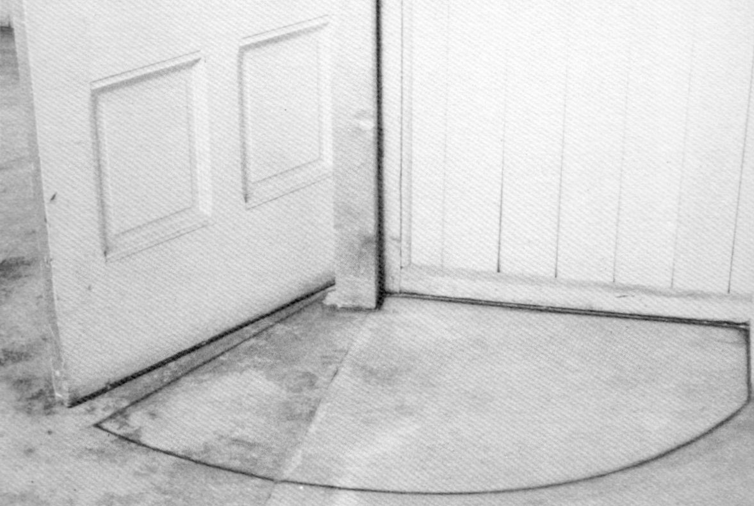

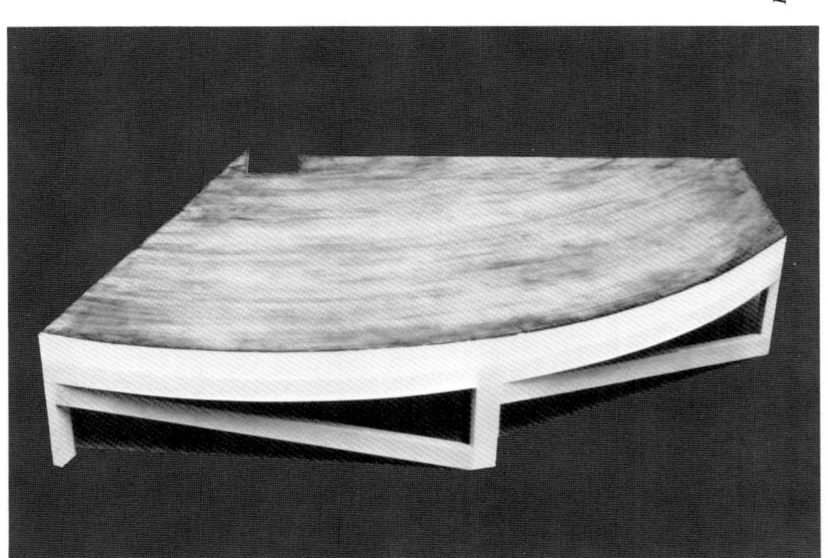

removed from the illusionistic set designs of Hollywood, which they imitate. ¶ The issue of theatricality in the visual arts has been hotly debated since Happenings in the early sixties. In subsequent criticism of Minimal Art, there was some mention of the theatrical effect of installations, in which the individual works of art had prop-like presences. Michael Fried's infamous attempt to equate Minimal sculpture and theatre treats works of art as actors with anthropomorphic qualities. These sculptures present a temporal situation designed specifically for an audience. In contrast to modernist painting, Fried sees Minimal Art as public, having no real aesthetic existence without a beholder. Fried concludes that, like theatre, Minimal Art is not art at all, but something between the arts.[7] In response, Donald Kuspit proposed that artists turned to theatricality to escape the limitations of formalism and, by so doing, reasserted

the potency of the imagination.[8] All of
the above interpretations come to bear
on Lere's work and locate him in a
tradition inspired by what Jack
Burnham has called a "post-formalist
sensibility." Burnham specifically has
translated Fried's concept of theatricality into his own idea of "systems
aesthetics," which "goes beyond a concern with staged environments and
happenings; it deals in a revolu-
tionary fashion with the larger problem
of boundary concepts."[9] Lere's transi-
tion from the theatrical architecture
to the "Water Suites" and "Sympathetic Structures" of the 1980s took a
comparable course.

¶ The shift in Lere's work is chronicled
in two major monuments: *Dowser
Fountain* and *Apsides House. Dowser
Fountain* of 1979 relates to all of the
previous "stages" and, like them, is
raised eleven inches from the floor by a
series of vertical and diagonal struts.
The large platform supports a concrete

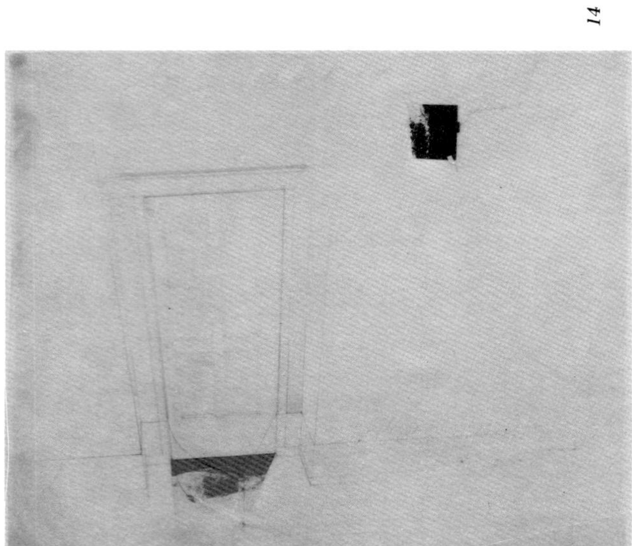

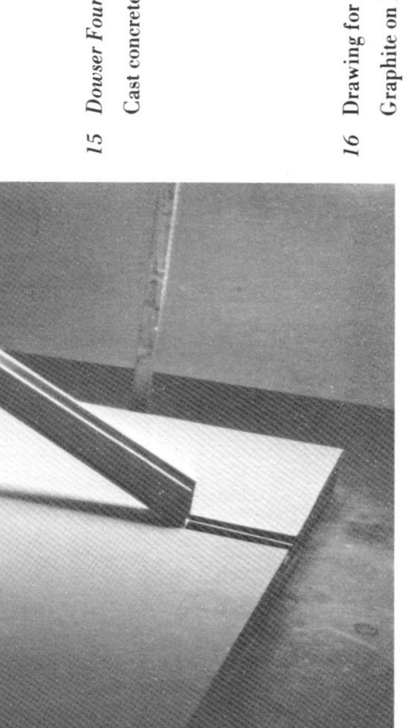

15 *Douser Fountain*, 1979
Cast concrete and wood, 60 x 192 x 192 in.

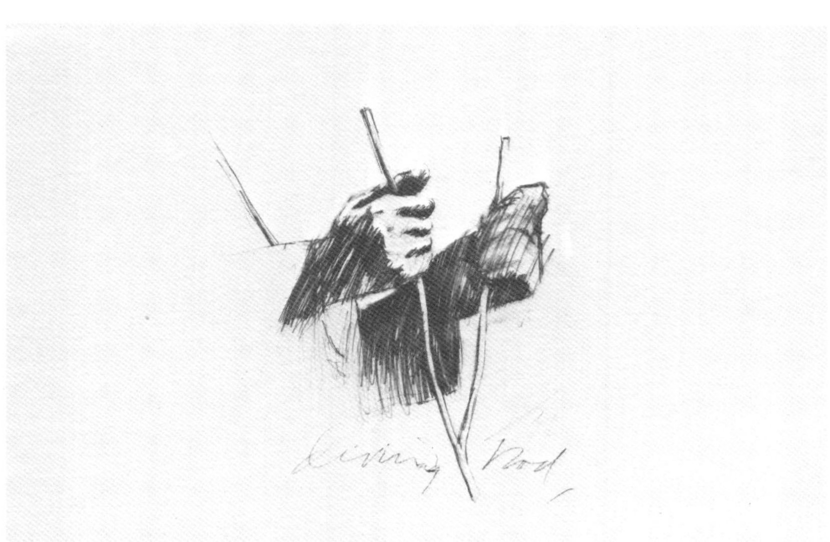

16 Drawing for a divining rod, 1984
Graphite on Herculene, 16 x 24 in.

fountain—a stylized, water-seeking divining rod. Two troughs indicate the flow of water, and an incised arc suggests the pivot of the fountain. At stake is not only the theatricality of the divining act but, more significantly, the fluidity of water and the description of systems for locating, containing, organizing and dispersing the vital substance.

¶ In one sense, *Dowser Fountain* dead ends in *The Big Bang Theory*, an outdoor series of troughs and ramps punctuated by elements of the future "Water Suites." *The Big Bang Theory* is the last of the theatrical architectures, one in which a kind of disconnection occurs. In the *Monument to the Southern Hemisphere*, Lere proposed a much more coherent tower-like structure, on whose exterior water drains counter-clockwise as it does in the Southern Hemisphere. Like *Dowser Fountain*, this monument inverts a natural system, which, as the artist

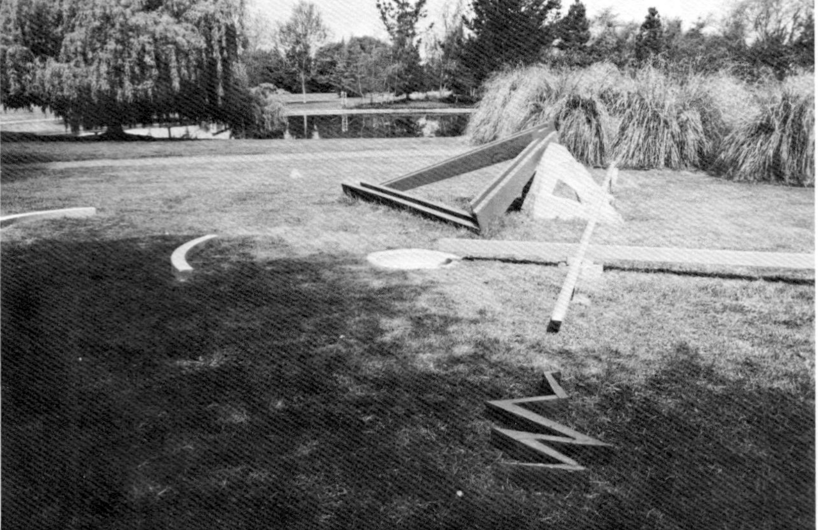

17 *Big Bang Theory*, 1982
Mixed media installation, Sonoma State University,
California. Dismantled.

explains, "theoretically is supposed to flip the world upside down just by reversing some small little action."

¶ *Apsides House* concluded the series of "stages" and introduced the circular structures: *Blackwater* of 1981, *Cyclatron* of 1982 and *Water Saw* of 1983. All of these led to *Halo/Wheel,* commissioned by The Museum of Contemporary Art in 1984. *Apsides House* makes articulate use of the building materials Lere used in his work of the seventies: plywood, tile, metal and concrete. A central dais is intersected by a track, on which a blackboard and ladder may slide. A huge circular ramp, broken by draining troughs, is tilted at an angle to perspectively suggest an ellipse, to which the title refers. (Apsides mark the points in an elliptical orbit that are nearest to and farthest from the center of attraction.) This sculpture represents the artist's first real consideration of installation and total manipulation of the gallery space. *Apsides House* filled its room at Mount St. Mary's College, Los Angeles, in 1980. It almost seemed to take up too much room. As a result, since it was ungraspable as a whole, the piece broke down into a series of relating elements. It was at this point that the artist realized that the dialogues between elements could be as interesting as the piece taken as a whole. It also signaled a shift in his thinking from concern with a public, theatrical space to a private, "metaphorical space."

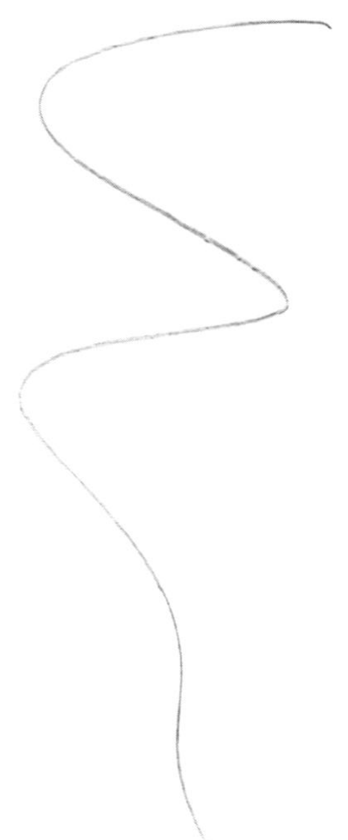

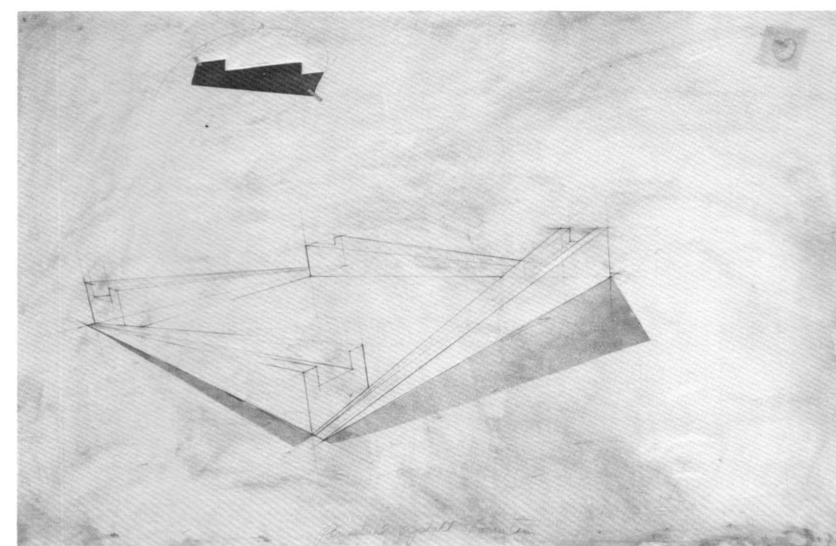

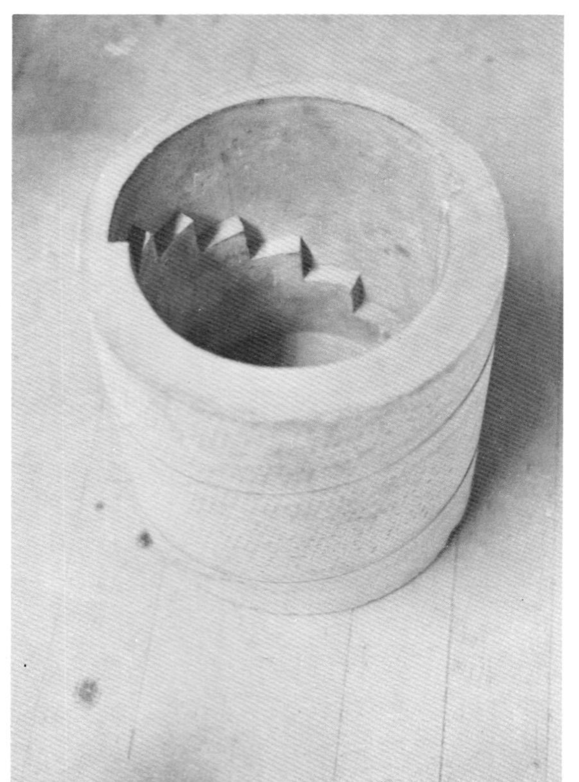

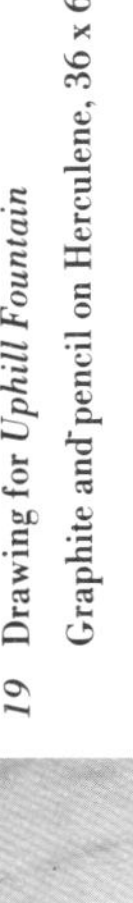

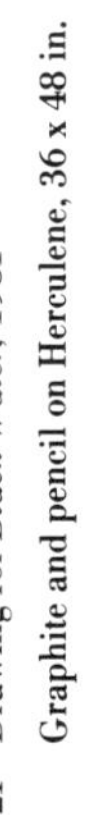

21 Drawing for *Black Water*, 1981
Graphite and pencil on Herculene, 36 x 48 in.

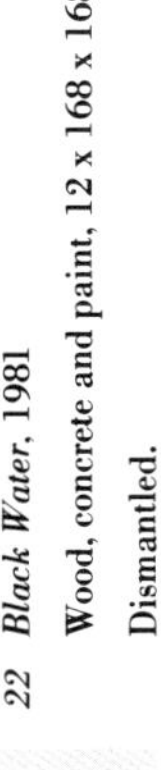

22 *Black Water*, 1981
Wood, concrete and paint, 12 x 168 x 168 in.
Dismantled.

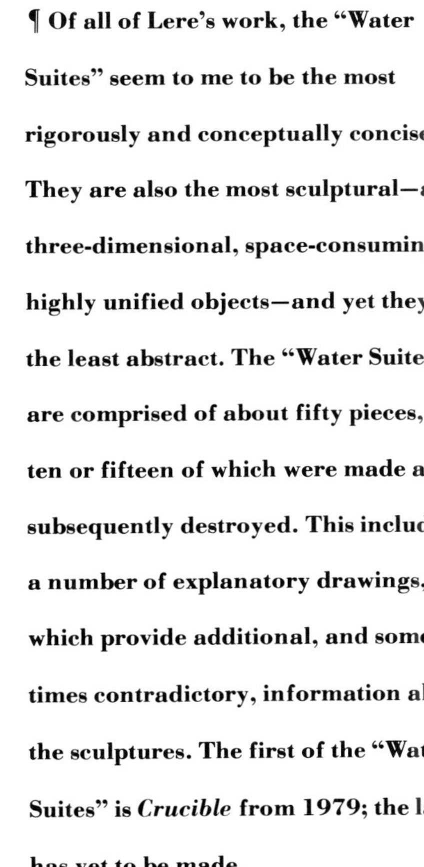

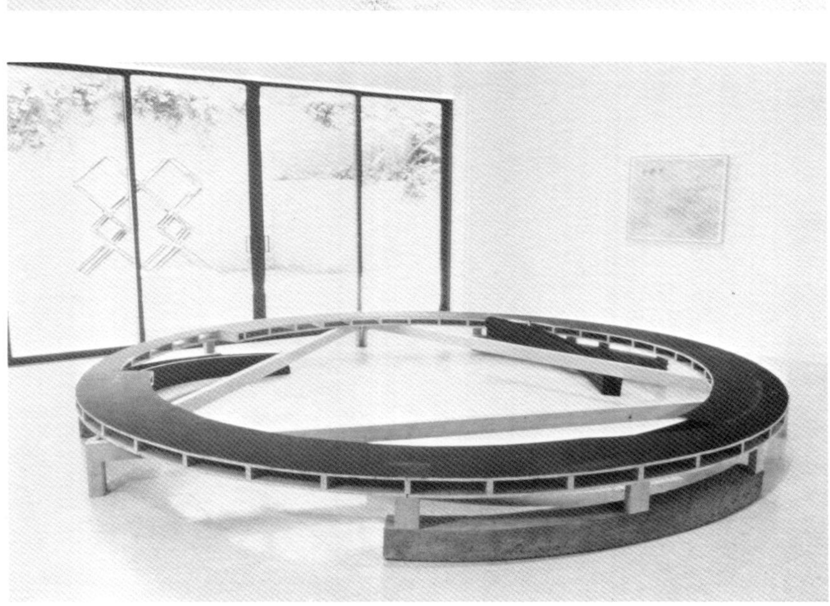

¶ Of all of Lere's work, the "Water Suites" seem to me to be the most rigorously and conceptually concise. They are also the most sculptural—as three-dimensional, space-consuming, highly unified objects—and yet they are the least abstract. The "Water Suites" are comprised of about fifty pieces, ten or fifteen of which were made and subsequently destroyed. This includes a number of explanatory drawings, which provide additional, and sometimes contradictory, information about the sculptures. The first of the "Water Suites" is *Crucible* from 1979; the last has yet to be made.

¶ The "Water Suites" differ from Lere's previous architectural constructions, although the sense of theatricality is still there. Rather than a tightly constructed, rational environment, an installation of the "Water Suites" consists of scattered, mostly low-lying, generally quirky objects. Most of them relate specifically to water or the move-

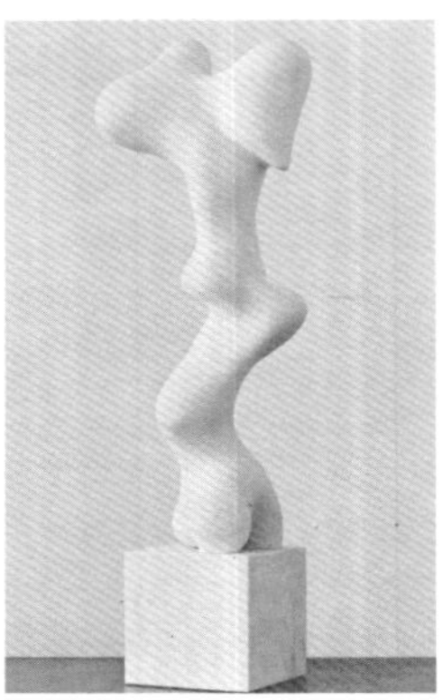

ment of liquids; the few that don't are morphologically similar to those that do. The imagery of the "Water Suites" can be discovered mostly in facts and pictures of natural phenomena and is indicative of Lere's ongoing interest in the natural sciences. He reads science magazines rather than art magazines, and non-fiction more frequently than fiction.

¶ The impulse to work from nature is as old as art itself but has never been more pointedly expressed than in this remark by the sculptor Julio Gonzalez: ——— Freestanding sculpture first appeared in the West, after the decline of ancient Greece, in Renaissance fountains. Before the twentieth century, sculpture in the round was primarily restricted to representations of the human body. Isolated landscape and non-human imagery belong to our century. Brancusi and Arp, especially, were concerned with sculpting the elemental aspects of nature. In their work, as in

One will not produce great art in making perfect circles with the aid of a compass and ruler, or in drawing one's inspiration from New York skyscrapers. The truly novel works, which often look bizarre, are, quite simply, those which are directly inspired by *Nature*.[10]

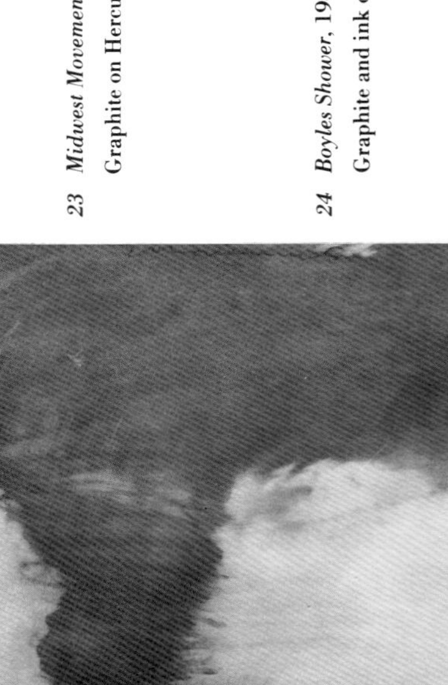

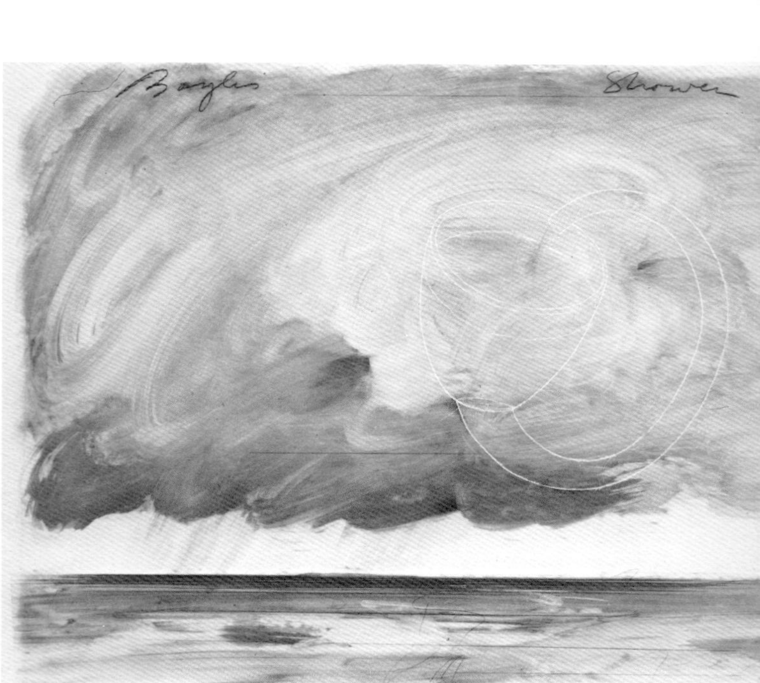

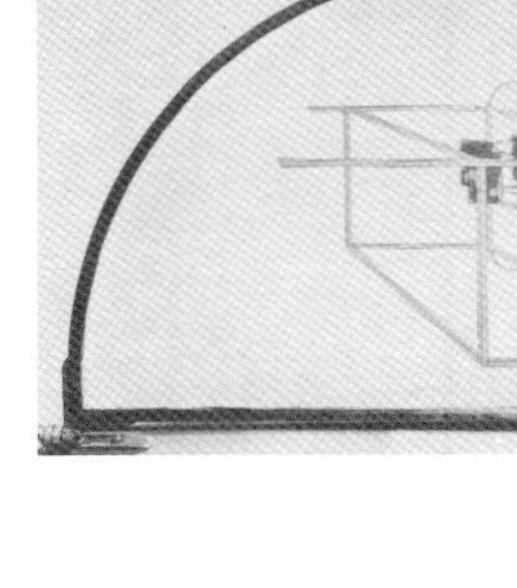

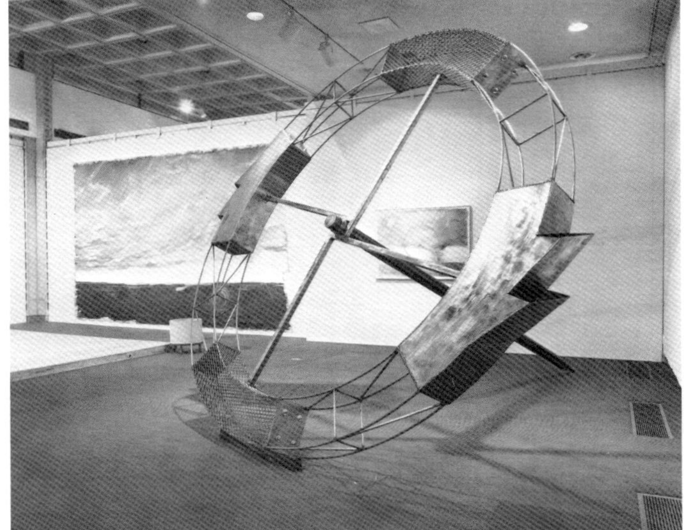

Lere's, one senses a passionate respect for nature. Lere grew up in North Dakota and Colorado, where the Great Plains stretch to what seems like in-finity—a vast, enveloping environment of sky and earth. His sculpture reflects that breadth and sparsity.

¶ Water is a basic element of nature, life-sustaining and refreshing, vital to our existence. From the earliest of times, its image has been evoked in philosophy, literature and art. The ancient Greek philosopher Thales believed everything to be made of water. It was the original substance, he thought, from which all others were formed. In our century, Marcel Duchamp depended considerably on water as a meaningful symbol in his work. Alchemical interpretations of Duchamp's work lean heavily on water as one of the four elements, an idea to which Lere's *Crucible* also refers. The waterfall is particularly significant in Duchamp's *Large Glass, Etant Donnés,* and *Water Mill within a Glider (In Neighboring Metals).* This last work depicts a water wheel, which one can-not help but associate with Lere's *Water Saw.* Potential movement is a shared theme, with water as the vital source of energy. Hans Haacke, among other contemporary artists, has used actual water in his work, maintaining that "water is the most living of inorganic substances" and asserting the basic, vital, elemental quality of the fluid.[11]

¶ The absence of water is the subject of the *Drains* and empty *Wells.* As structures promoting the passage of liquid, Lere offers the *Crucibles* and the *Monument to the Southern Hemisphere.* Metaphorically capable of moving through water are the boat shapes and *Water Saw. Split Stream* and *Opposing Stream* suggest the flow of water, nature in flux. The philosopher Heraclitus, a century after Thales, called on the image of water to express his belief that everything constantly changes: you can never step in the same stream twice.

¶ Lere's streams are captured, solidified and rendered useless in plaster and concrete, water-based materials. Cold cast bronze is the only unnatural material he has used in the "Water Suites." It specifically contrasts with and emphasizes the other natural materials. The different steels used in *Water Saw* (cold-rolled), the *Vortices* (mild) and *Crucible* (galvanized) impart

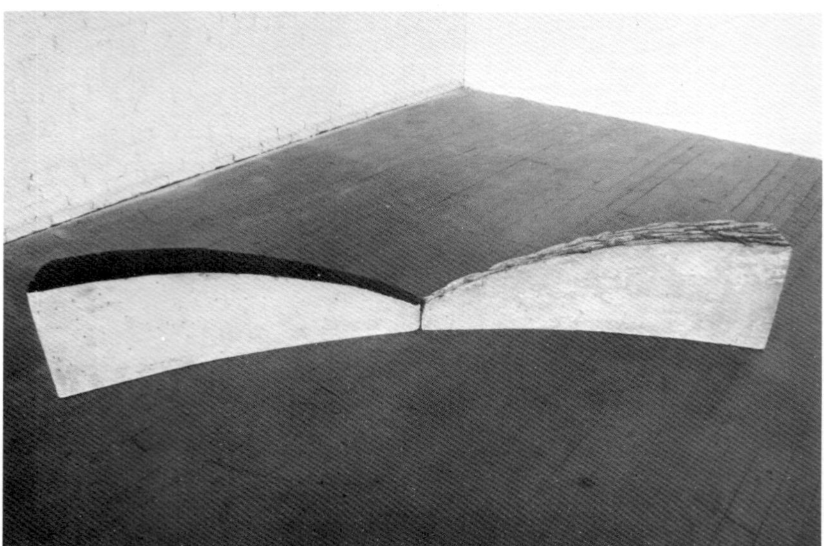

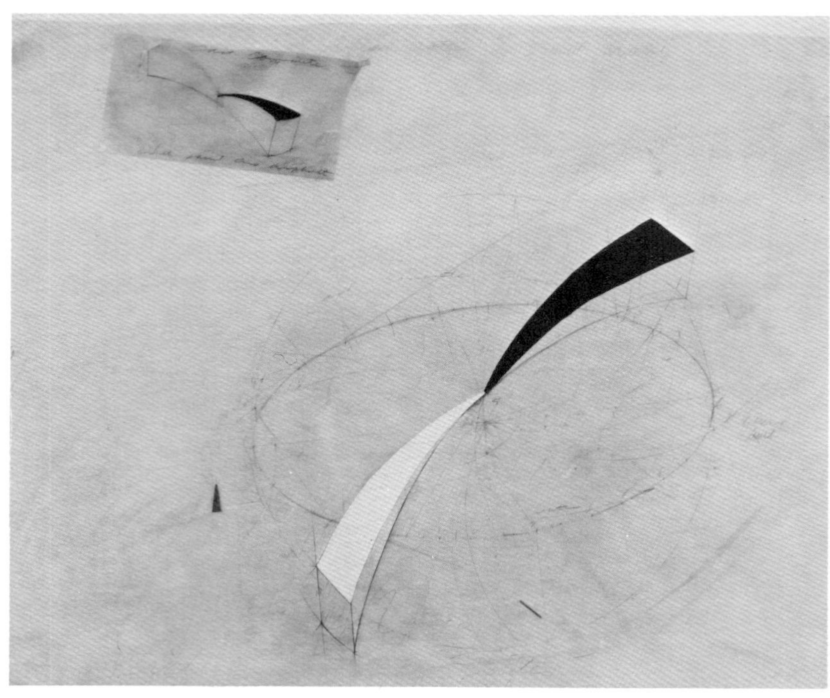

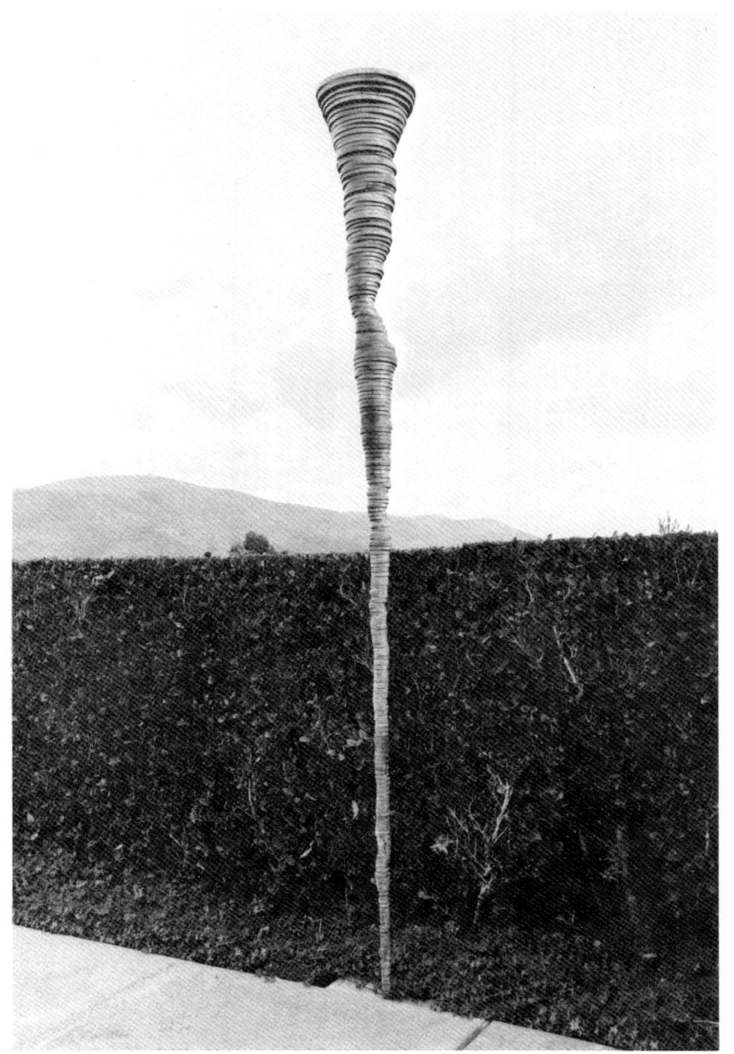

28 *Standing Vortex,* 1984
Plated steel, 109 x 12 in.

to each image a cool elegance, adding

to the somewhat impersonal demeanor

of installations of the "Water Suites."

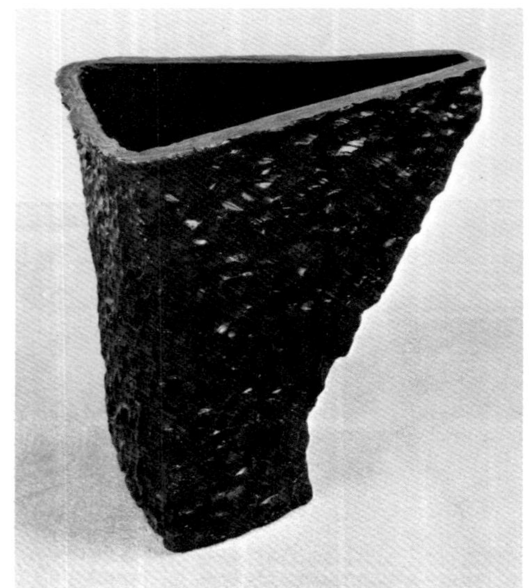

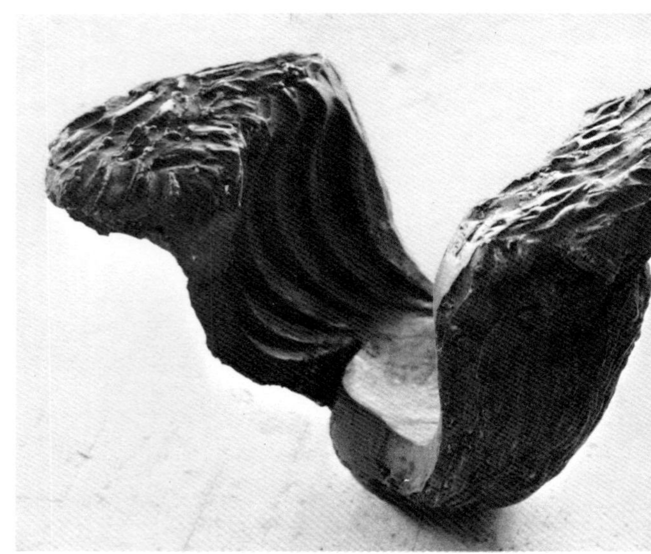

29 *Cistern*, 1984
Cold cast bronze, 18 x 12 x 16 in.

30 *Water Wings*, 1983
Plaster and graphite, 18 x 24 in.

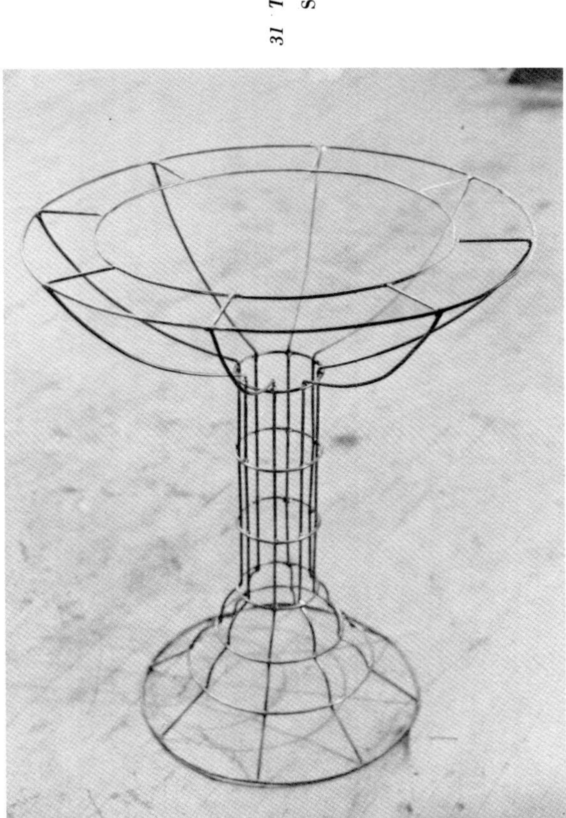

31 *Transparent Fountain*, 1983
Steel, 32 x 24 x 24 in.

J Paolo Uccello. *Perspective Study of a Chalice*,
c. 1430–40
Pen and ink, 13½ x 9½ in.

¶ The "Water Suites" are, with a few exceptions, rather small, apparently portable: human size or less. As Robert Morris has noted, the smaller the object, the more intimate, more private it seems.[12] Sculpture that is very different in size from the thing it represents will, according to the aesthetician F. David Martin, "be more physically present, more of our world," by establishing a psychological tension through scale.[13] The psychological impact of the "Water Suites" is increased dialectically by playing positive against negative, open against solid and fluid against rigid. *Fountain*, for example, is transparent, outlined in wire—a drawing in space— and cannot contain or circulate water. The *Drains* are negative molds "containing" the form of water as it empties into or through a drain. *Split Stream* is opaque rather than clear like water. These simple conceptual maneuvers increase the tension.

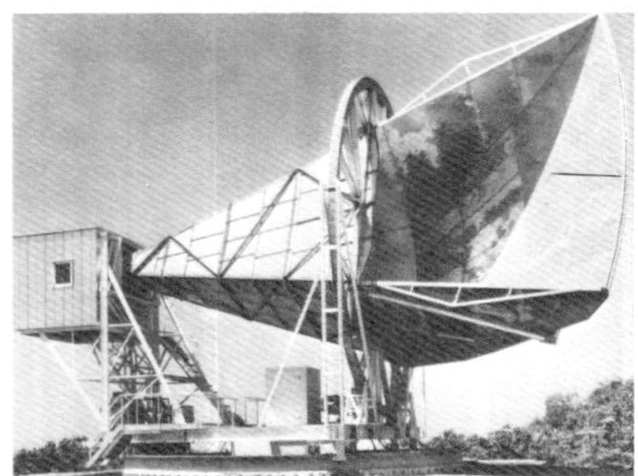

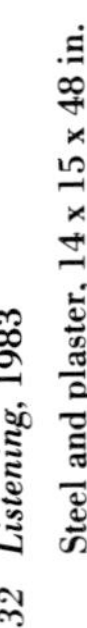

¶ Lere's interest in natural phenomena and systems supports the claim for the conceptual basis of his work. Like Haacke and Oppenheim, Lere interprets and amplifies certain systems, an approach different from, say, Sol LeWitt's, in which systems are used to structure the form of a work of art. The natural systems, or "movements in nature," Lere appropriates include the tornado and the draining of water. Artificial circulation of water, illustrated by the *Fountains* and *Water Saw,* scientific systems, such as the radio-telescope mimicked in *Listening,* and the magical science of alchemy suggest the range of Lere's thinking in the "Water Suites." The individual sculptures are not scientific demonstrations, but aesthetic interpretations of aspects of natural science.

¶ Lere insightfully characterizes all of his sculptures as props or tools. The "stages" make specific reference to theatrical props, while the megaphone-

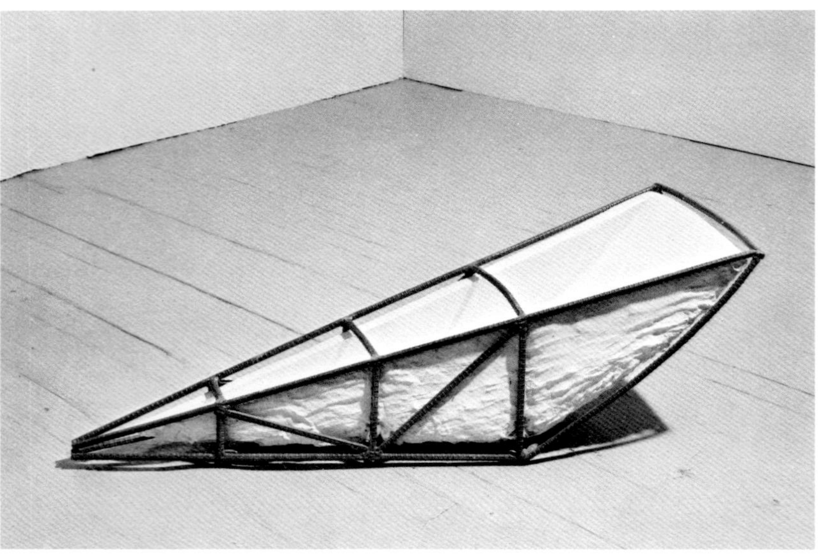

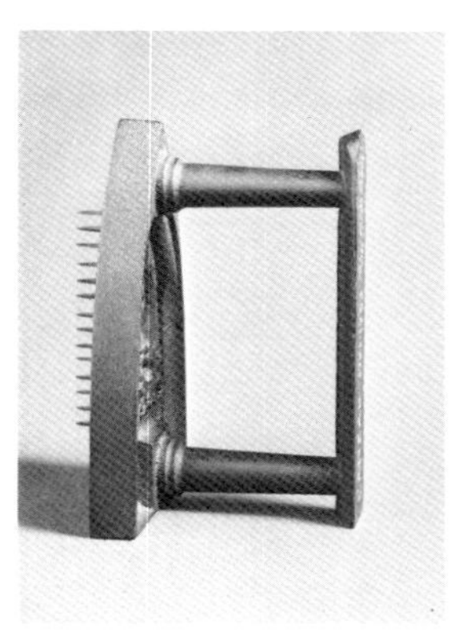

33 *Half Truths*, 1982
Enamel on wood and plaster, 30 x 14 in. diameter

L Man Ray. *Cadeau*, 1963
Mixed media, 5½ x 3½ x 3½ in.

like *Half Truths* and the device for *Listening* suggest the possibility of use. Intertwined with this notion of prop or tool is the subversion of conventional certainties. For example, *Dowser Fountain* seeks rather than spouts water, and the construction of *Half Truths* actually prevents one from speaking through it. These are, as Lere has said, "functionless tools." The contradiction is doubled by his consideration, in the first place, of works of art as useful objects. As a rule, aesthetic objects are differentiated from other things in the world by their non-practical, non-functional nature. Like a double negative, this definitive characteristic of art works is demonstrated by a kind of conceptual game-playing.

¶ The idea of apparent but negated function recalls the contradictions implicit in Dada. What would happen if one were to iron with the tack-studded surface of Man Ray's *Cadeau* or to measure with Duchamp's arbitrary and

irregular *3 Standard Stoppages?* The
juxtaposition of function and non-
function results in a serious humor.
This is not to suggest that either the
Dadaists' or Lere's work is particularly
funny. It does call to my mind, though,
Robert Smithson's marvelous discus-
sion of the fourth-dimensional "ha-ha"
concept, illustrated by certain artists of
the 1960s and "the highly ordered
nonsense of Lewis Carroll."[14] At stake is
really Smithson's own brand of poetic
nonsense in his appropriation of types
of laughter (the chuckle, the giggle,
the snicker, etc.) as models for various
methods of structural order in art.
¶ One of Mark Lere's favorite works
of art is Robert Morris's *Box With The
Sound of Its Own Making* of 1961.
From a small wooden cube come the
tape-recorded sounds of the box being
sawed and nailed together. Like many
of Morris's Neo-Dada objects, the *Box*
is humorous, while illustrating the most
serious aspect of the artist's oeuvre:

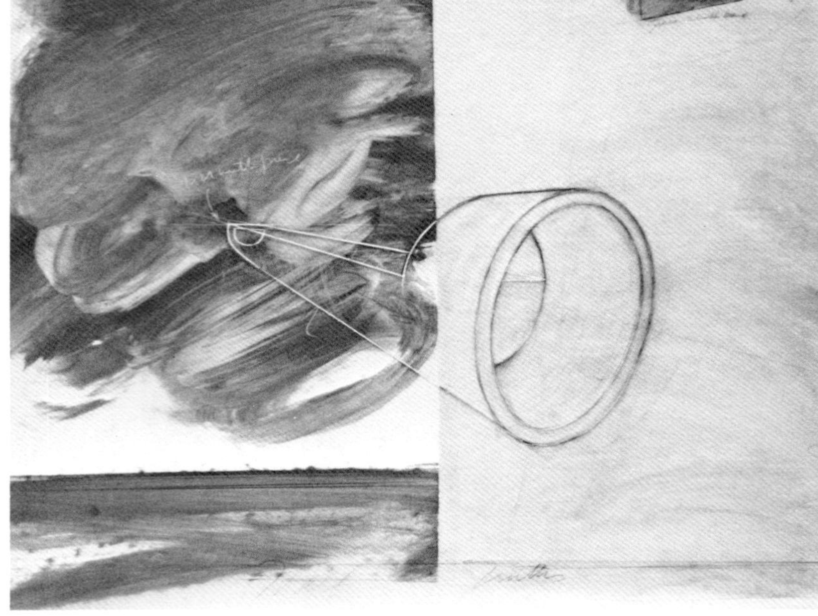

*34 Drawing for Half Truths, 1984
Graphite on Herculene, 28 x 32 in.*

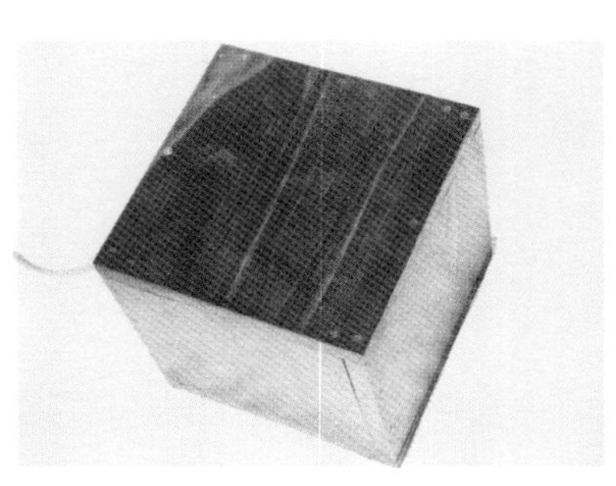

35 *Jigsaw Landscape*, 1984
Paint on plywood, 96 x 120 in.

M Robert Morris. *A Box with the Sound of its own Making*, 1961
Wood, 12 x 12 x 12 in.

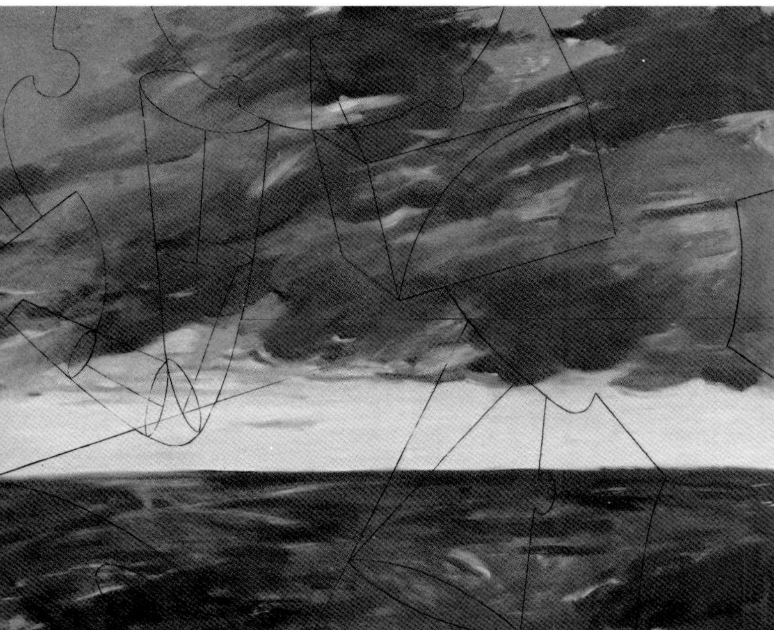

his egocentric concern with process. On the other hand, Lere cites the example of William Wegman's photography as work with a great sense of humor and has commented upon significant analogies between art and comedy. —————————————— By avoiding literal representation and substituting suggestion and implication, generally more poetic than humorous, Lere seduces and provokes his audience. Mystery, futility and juxtaposition provide the "structure about discovery" he associates with the punchline of a joke. "When it happens, all of a sudden you understand. You have a new insight."

I think there's a heavy relationship between comedy—perfect good stand-up comedy—and very good artwork. It has to do with timing, not in the sense of when somebody does something, but the timing of a person seeing it and understanding what it's about. Whether the piece is humorous or not, the timing element is still there: the amount of information that's given as opposed to the amount of information that isn't.

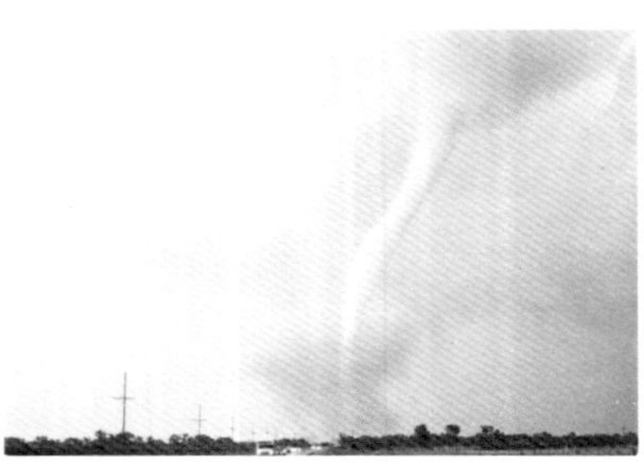

¶ In a series of drawings entitled "Midwest Movements," Lere first proposed the conceptual associations that would be materially demonstrated in the "Sympathetic Structures." In one drawing, a dancing couple is accompanied by a tornado. In another, the whirling funnel is related to a cat chasing its tail. The "Midwest Movements" represent for Lere the sober sensibility and homespun wisdom of Midwesterners, based on axiomatic associations. In these drawings, the names of which derive from cliches or superstitions, Lere synchronizes a set of native convictions with a weather system which dominates and regulates life in the Midwest.

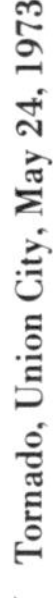

36 *Midwest Movements*, 1983
Dry wall cut-out, 18 x 9 in. Dismantled.

37 *Tornado Drawing*, 1984
Graphite on Herculene, 20 x 30 in.

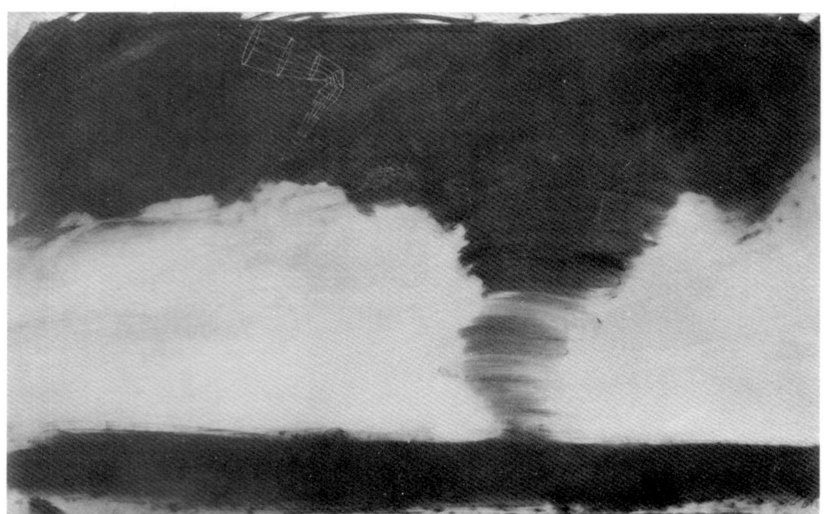

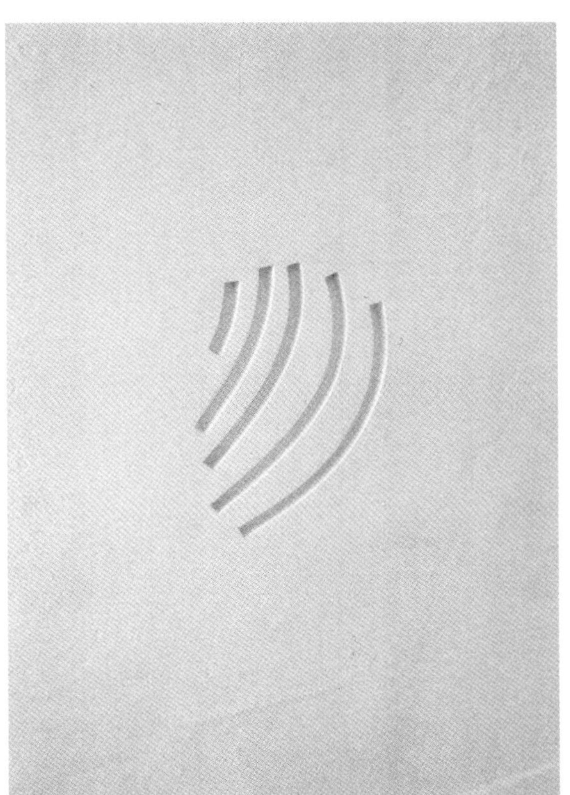

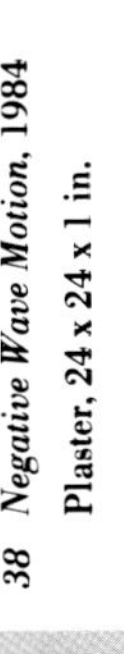

38 *Negative Wave Motion,* 1984
Plaster, 24 x 24 x 1 in.

39 *Tornado Wall Depression,* 1984
Plaster, 48 x 32 x 2 in.

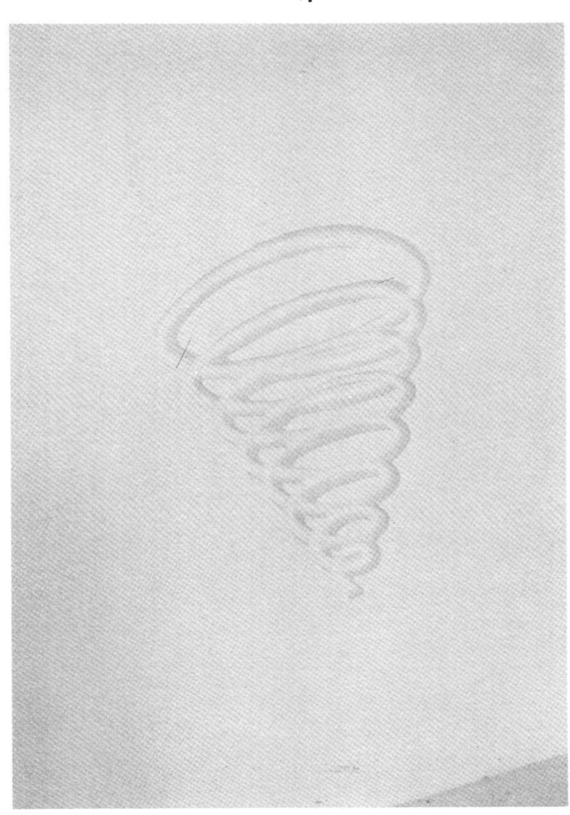

¶ The "Sympathetic Structures" grew
from and include a number of the
"Water Suites." They do not constitute
a series but suggest certain relationships between individual objects in a
group, based primarily on shape. The
plaster *Drain*, for example, relates
obviously to the steel *Sieve*. Inside the
vaguely trapezoidal *Well* is a series of
tiny steps. The wax *Steps* invert and
make positive the inside of the empty
Well. The solid water from *Black Spout*
likewise echoes the volume of the *Well*.
Listening and *Half Truths* relate conceptually as well as in terms of mor-
phological identification.

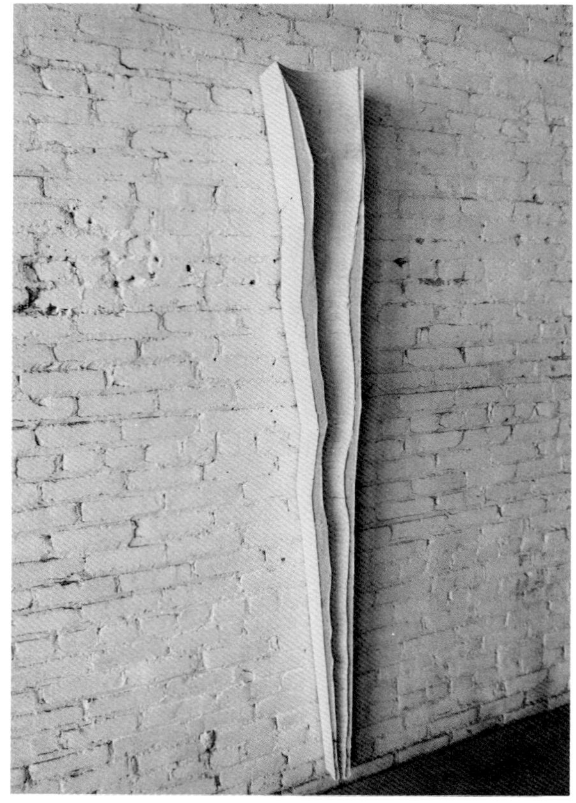

40 Untitled, 1982
Cast plaster, 88 x 6 x 8 in.

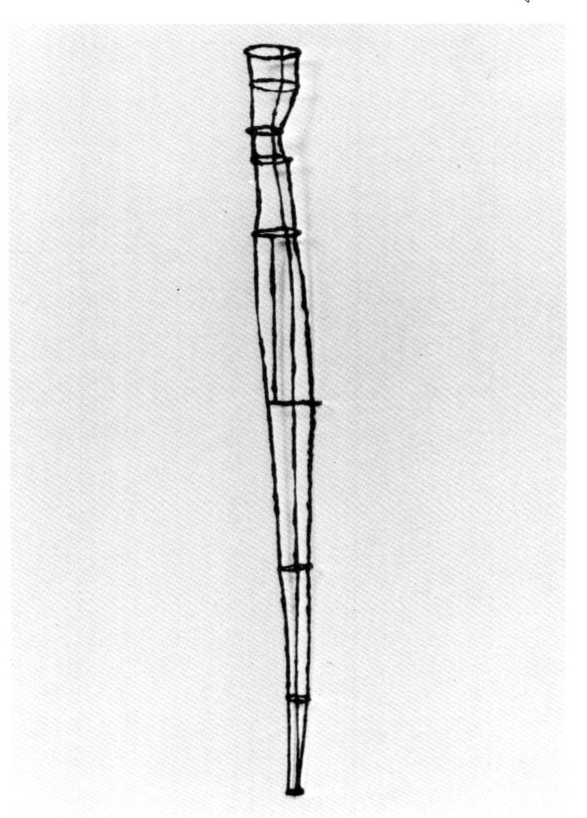

41 *Prosthesis*, 1984
Steel and wax, 70 x 6 x 6 in.

¶ As an aspect of the "Sympathetic Structures," metamorphosis is illustrated by the conceptual transformation of the *Crucible* into the boat shape. This is extended and concretized in the proposal for *House/Boat*, in which a house shape becomes a boat. An anthropomorphic translation is evident in the relationship of *Vortex* and *Prosthesis*. The leg-form is specifically linked to the attenuated, vertical funnel of a tornado. The configuration of *Prosthesis* was in fact suggested to the artist by a photograph of a tornado. Through identification and transformation, the "Sympathetic Structures" illustrate Lere's belief that "each new work alters the meaning of the previous one. The first piece explains the second one."

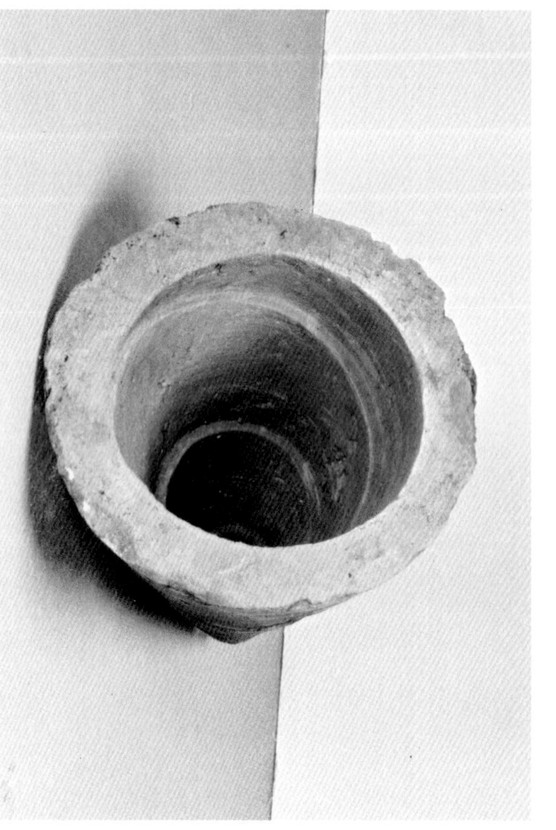

42 *House Boat*, 1983
Pencil and graphite on paper, 20 x 30 in.

43 *Drain*, 1980
Cast concrete, 36 x 36 in.

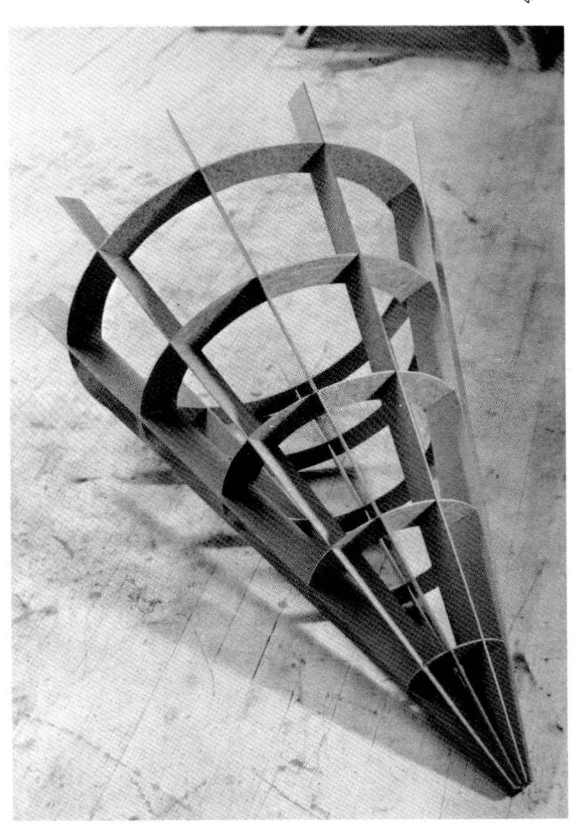

44 *Seive*, 1983
Masonite, 36 x 48 x 36 in.

¶ The arrangement of elements in an installation of the "Water Suites" is determined to an extent by the "Sympathetic Structures." Objects are carefully located so that appropriate associations are apparent. Although the gallery floor is often broken into a series of levels, the works are not elevated on bases. The low-lying objects require a reorientation of our viewing habits. As Robert Morris has pointed out,———— We expect to encounter objects which will block our vision at a relatively close range. Seeing is directed straight out, 90° to the wall or at an object never far from a wall. The pervasive spatial context is one of room space with its strongly accentuated divisions between vertical and horizontal and the subsequent emphasis on orientations of plumb and level.[15] Lere subverts not only the implied vertical grid (by encouraging us to look down at and into) but the horizontal grid, through a seemingly random scattering of objects on the floor. The scattering is strategic, however, so that the viewer is led into and directed through what Lere calls the "mine field" of sculpture.

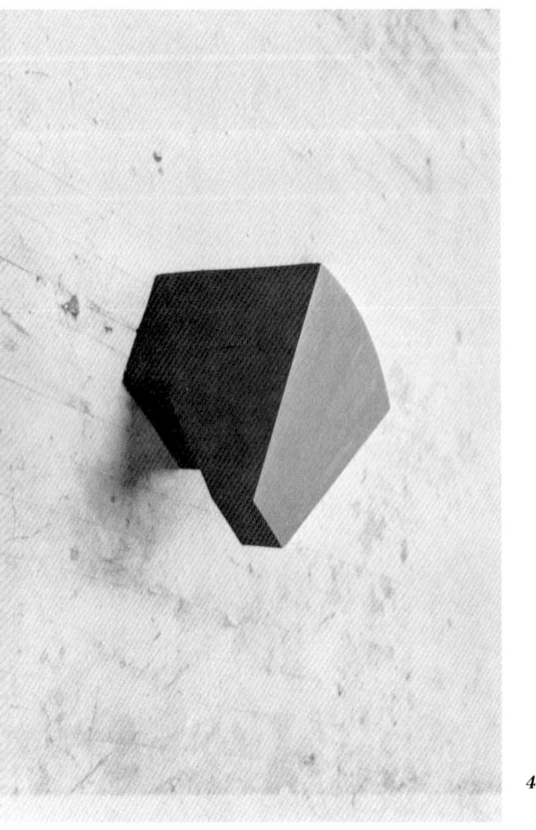

45 *Wax Well*, 1983
Wax, 18 x 16 x 12 in.

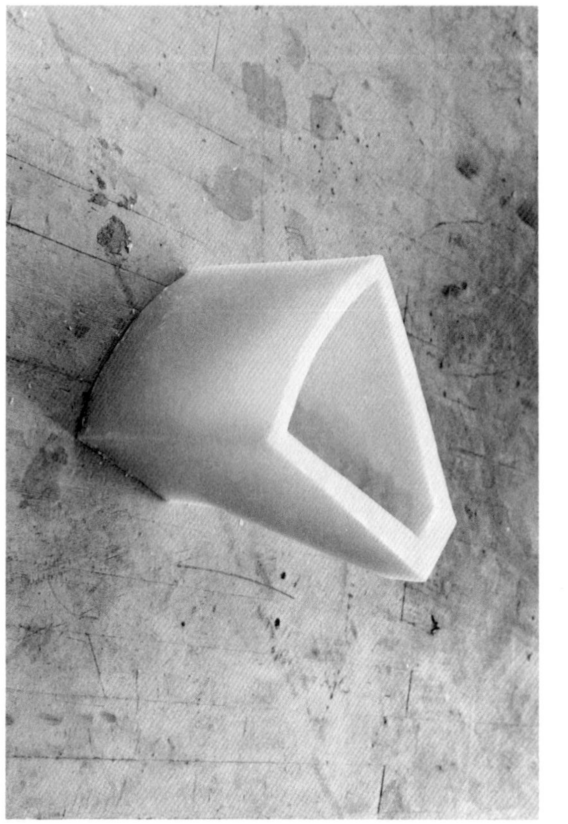

46 *Black Spout*, 1983
Blackboard paint on wood, 16 x 16 x 12 in.

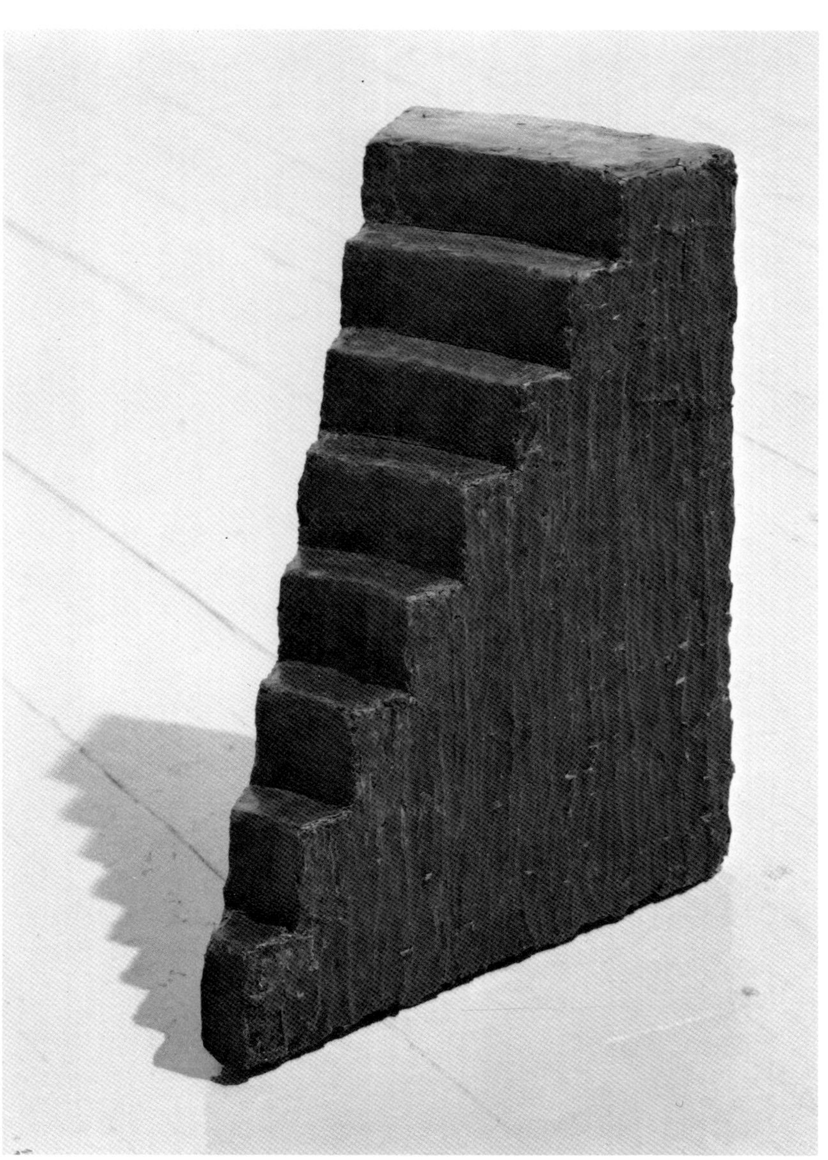

47 Wax Steps, 1984
Wood and wax, 16 x 12 x 8 in.

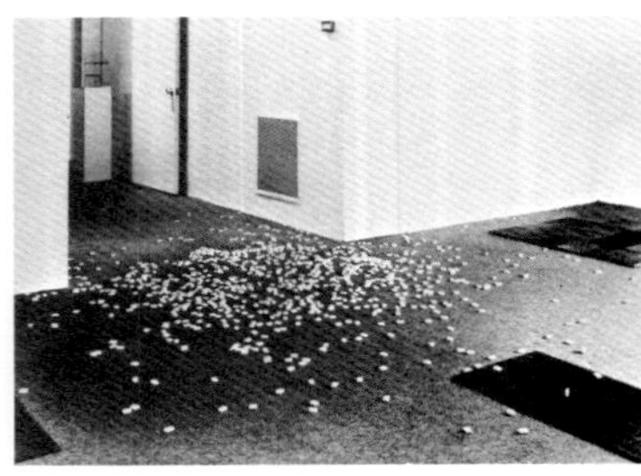

O Carl Andre. *Spill (Scatter Piece)*, 1966
800 plastic blocks and canvas bag

¶ Carl Andre's *Spill (Scatter Piece)* of 1966 set a precedent for random structure, soon completely appropriated by process artists. Lere was particularly influenced by Barry Le Va's "Distribution Pieces," which were inspired by the materials scattered in the sculptor's studio. Lere too found that what was most interesting was the way the work linked in the studio in various states of completion and finish. For the sculptor, the studio is especially the sculptor, the studio is especially important in determining the spatial orientation of objects, since he works in real rather than illusionistic space. As F. David Martin has shown, the positioning of things in terms of "up-down, left-right, and near-far" requires a system of reference with "a configurational center . . . a place that is a gathering point around which a field of interests is structured." For the farmer, he continues, the configurational center is his farm; for the

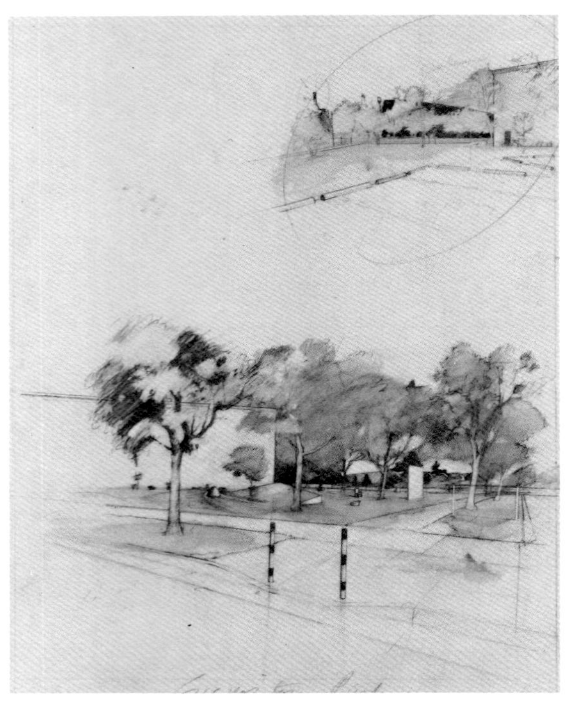

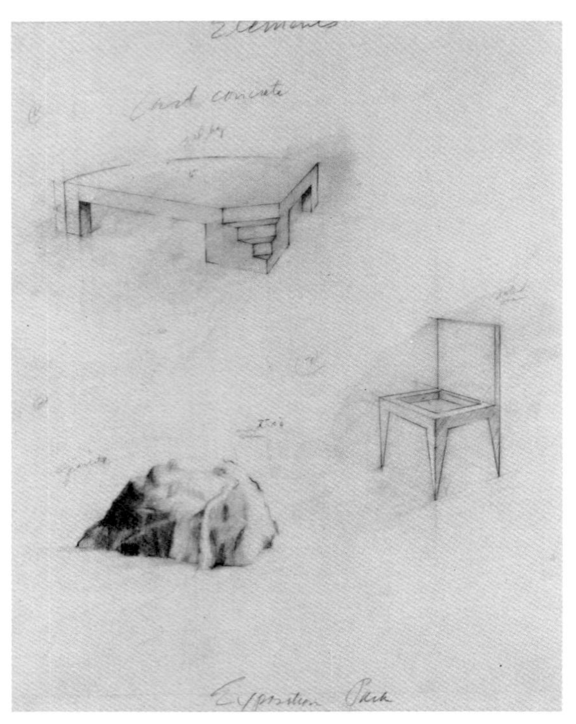

48-51 Four drawings for *Exposition Park*, 1982
Graphite on Herculene, 36 x 24 in. each

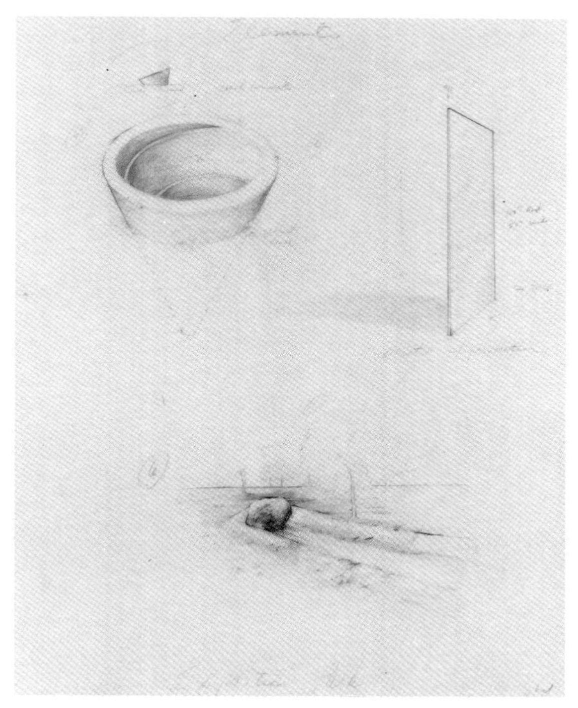

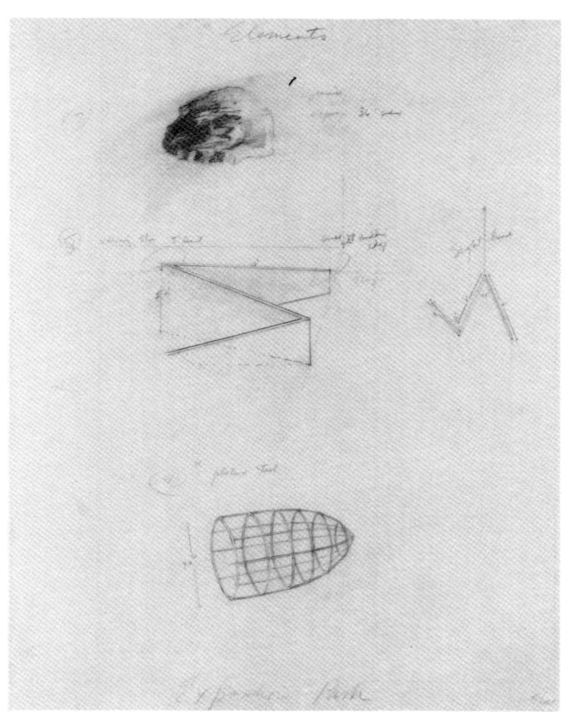

Roman, Rome. "With sculptors the configurational center is usually the studio and its environs."[16] All this is not to suggest that Lere reproduces his studio in the gallery, but that the casual arrangement of the "Water Suites" duplicates the artist's intellectual and artistic studio decisions.

¶ Lere's interest in the scattered installation extends to the recent outdoor projects: *Seattle Scatter* and *Halo/ Wheel.* In these, random scattering is regimented and superceded by large-scale mapping. Scattering suggests disarray; mapping, a superimposed order. The outdoor pieces are spread across their respective cities. In Los Angeles, the twelve sites mark points on two concentric circles whose center is The Museum of Contemporary Art; *Seattle Scatter's* five sites mark the corners of a pentagonal boat shape. The form is conceptually apparent once the plan or map is known. Obviously, the sculptures cannot be perceived simultane-

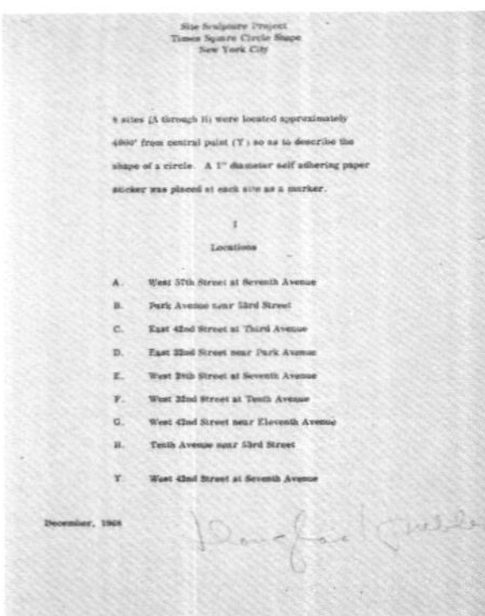

Site Sculpture Project
Times Square Circle Shape
New York City

8 sites (A through H) were located approximately
4000' from central point (Y) so as to describe the
shape of a circle. A 1" diameter self adhering paper
sticker was placed at each site as a marker.

I

Locations

A.   West 57th Street at Seventh Avenue

B.   Park Avenue near 53rd Street

C.   East 42nd Street at Third Avenue

D.   East 22nd Street near Park Avenue

E.   West 29th Street at Seventh Avenue

F.   West 32nd Street at Tenth Avenue

G.   West 42nd Street near Eleventh Avenue

H.   Tenth Avenue near 53rd Street

Y   West 42nd Street at Seventh Avenue

December, 1968

P   Douglas Huebler. *Site Sculpture Project* (detail), 1968

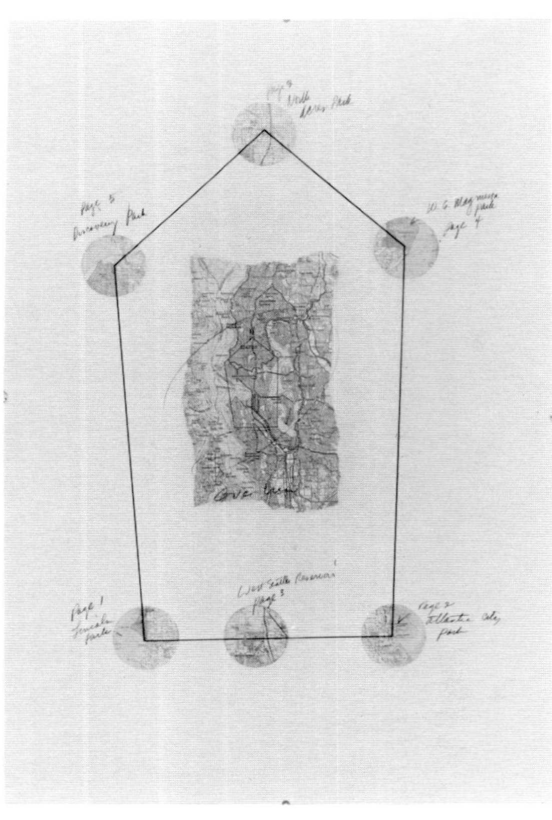

52   Drawing for *Seattle Scatter*, (overview map), 1980
Graphite on Herculene, 30 x 20 in.

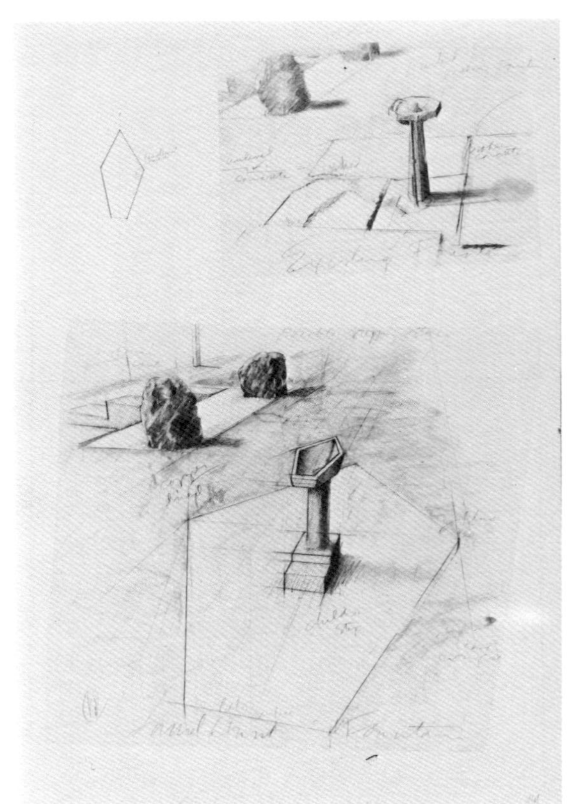

53   Drawing for *Seattle Scatter*, (Laurelhurst Fountain), 1980
Graphite on Herculene, 30 x 20 in.

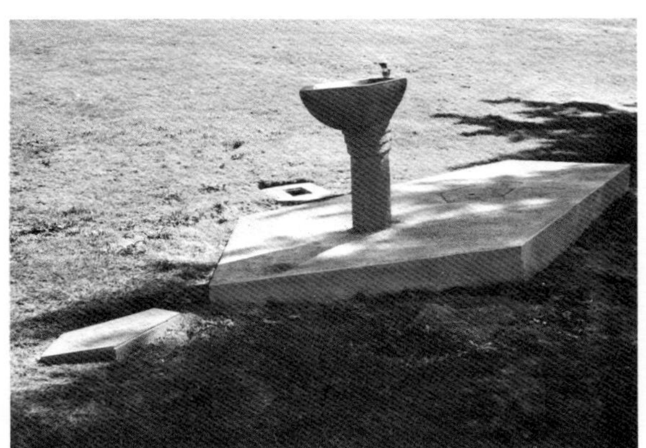

54   *Boat Fountain*, 1980
Slate and steel, 32 x 198 x 72 in.
Laurelhurst site, one of five permanent sites in Seattle, Washington

ously. This in essence reverses the motivation of the gallery installations, whose conceptual order is not static but alters as the pieces are experienced in juxtaposition.

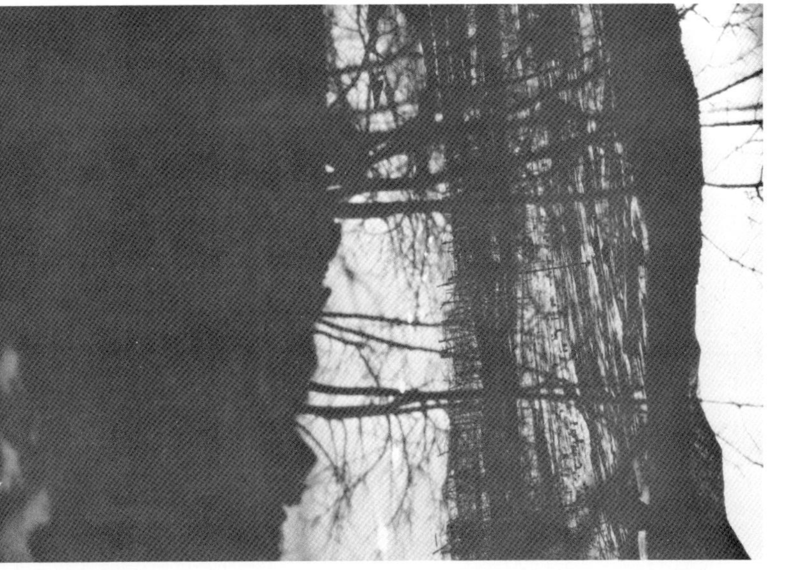

55 *County Line Neon*, 1970
Outdoor neon installation ¼ mile long. Dismantled.

56 Drawing for *County Line*, 1970
Graphite on Herculene, 24 x 12 in.

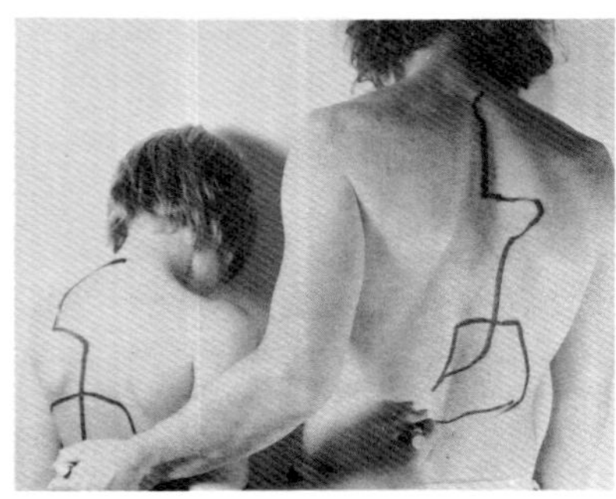

Q Dennis Oppenheim, Erik Oppenheim. *A Feed-back Situation*, Aspen, Colorado, July, 1971. "I originate the movement which Erik translates and returns to me. What I get in return is my movement fed through his sensory system." Dennis Oppenheim.

¶ **Examples of the conceptual maneu-vering involved in widely dispersed work include Artschwager's "blps" and Douglas Huebler's use, in the late six-ties, of small stickers to mark points in the urban environment. Huebler's work relies heavily on the mapping process as a principle of conceptual organization. Lere's interest in map-ping can be traced to his *County Line*, executed in 1970 while he was a student at Metropolitan State College in Denver. The broken line drawn to separate counties on a map was repro-duced in neon in the actual landscape between Clear Creek and Gilpin coun-ties. Dennis Oppenheim's *Time Line*, which traced in the snow the time zone boundary between Main and Canada, was certainly of interest to the younger artist. On a more intimate scale, both artists have "mapped" the human body: Oppenheim with his son Erik in 1971, and Lere in his book *Heavenly Bodies* of 1978.**

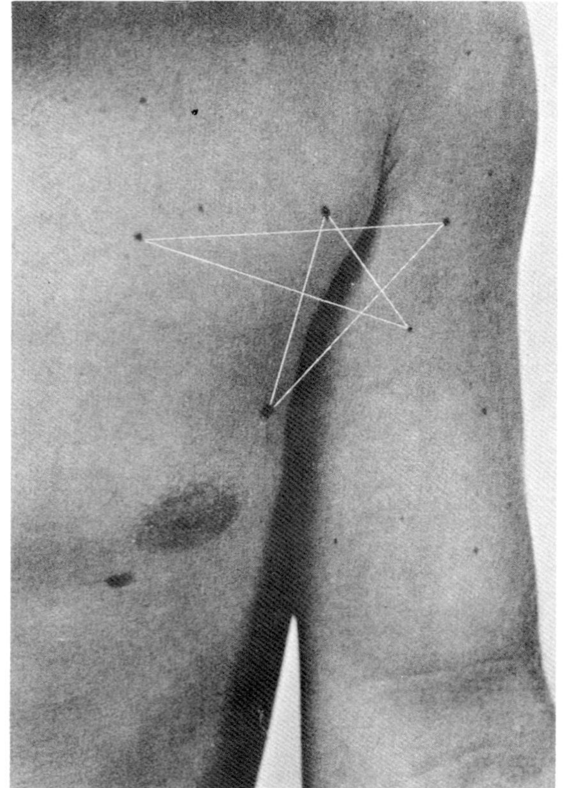

57 *Heavenly Bodies*, 1977
Self-published book

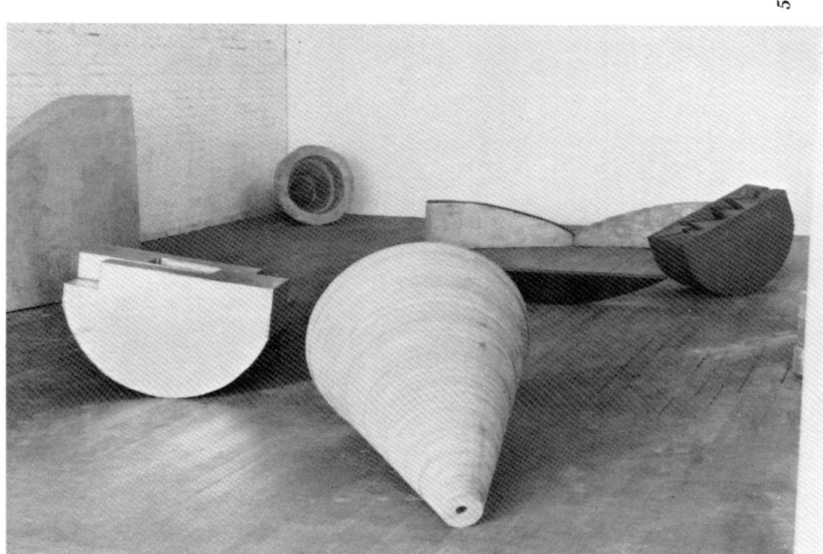

¶ Using the model of a map and its function as a symbol, Ludwig Wittgenstein and Susanne Langer have investigated the symbolic function of language. Lere's own thinking about the scattered installation and, within them, the internal relationships proposed by the "Sympathetic Structures," offers a comparibly feasible mode of interpretation. Lere suggests that each sculpture functions like a word. Five or six together make a sentence. The 1983 exhibitions of the "Water Suites" can be viewed as extensive paragraphs. The analogy holds for Lere since he deals with the sculptures as evidences of the creative process, with each object "standing for" a thought or idea.

¶ In terms of this linguistic analogy, a distinction is in order between semantics and syntax. Semantics, which is a study of the meanings of words, would in our case extend to the meanings of individual works of art. To continue the analogy, the "Sympathetic Structures" as a group derive their meaning from their syntax, i.e., their relational ordering within a given installation. Certainly relevant is the linguistic model of Structuralism, in which works of art are treated as a series of signs. The identities or meanings of the individual signs are determined by differentiation and comparison. The syntactical ordering of terms provides the context within which these terms are interpreted. According to Philip Pettit's survey of Structuralism, "The meaning of the whole depends on the meaning of its parts so that it changes if the meaning of any part changes . . . . The meaning of a part is determined by its background contrasts with what might have replaced it without making nonsense of the whole."[17] Jack Burnham's analysis is particularly relevant to the "Sympathetic Structures," since he recognizes in language the possibility "for shifts in the meaning of words according to contextual

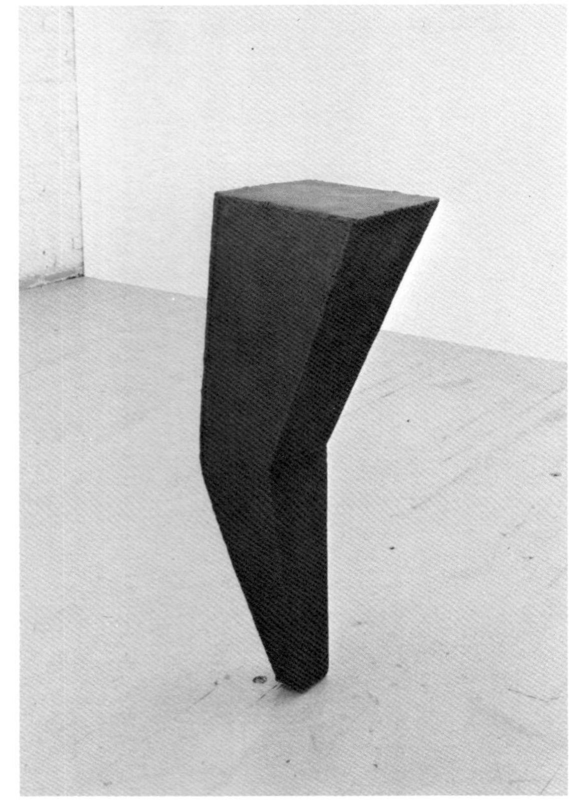

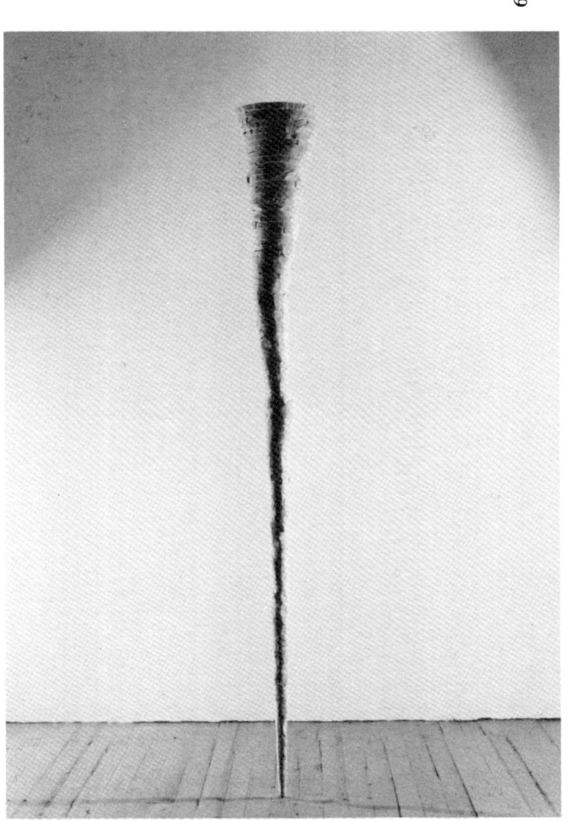

60 *Standing Vortex*, 1982
Particle board and steel, 92 x 12 x 12 in.

and positional arrangement."[18]

¶ While Structuralism extends the linguistic model to non-linguistic works of art, Burnham offers a distinction which should, I think, be taken far more seriously than has heretofore been the case. "All writings and strings of spoken words subjected to linguistic analysis are considered ordered and finite texts . . . . Analytically, visual works of art should be considered unordered but finite texts."[19] In language, *the linear order of words in a sentence determines its meaning.* Works of visual art, on the other hand, are spatial, not temporal. There is no specific program for reading the elements of one work of art or for viewing a series of works in an installation.

¶ Works of art are not signs, like words, whose meanings are determined by convention. No dictionary of art will ever disclose the meaning of either a single work or a series of related works. Langer has proposed that works

of art function as symbols rather than
signs. Pursuing the linguistic analogy,
she compares language, "the paragon
of symbolic form," to works of art.
While art is symbolic of human feeling, it does not constitute "a language
of feeling . . . because its elements are
not words—independent associative
symbols with a reference fixed by
convention . . . It is not a language,
because it has no vocabulary." Art
is *like* language, in that "what art
expresses is *not* actual feeling, but ideas
of feeling; as language does not express
actual things and events but ideas of
them."[20] Langer's analysis seems to me
relevant to the symbolic and metaphorical function of Lere's work. The
artist's assertion that the sculptural

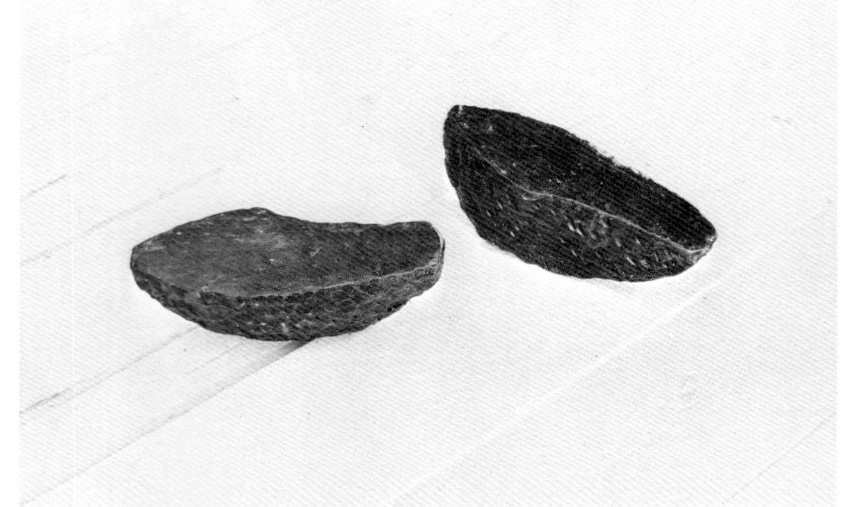

61 *Bronze Rocker*, 1984
Black bronze, 6 x 12 x 5 in.

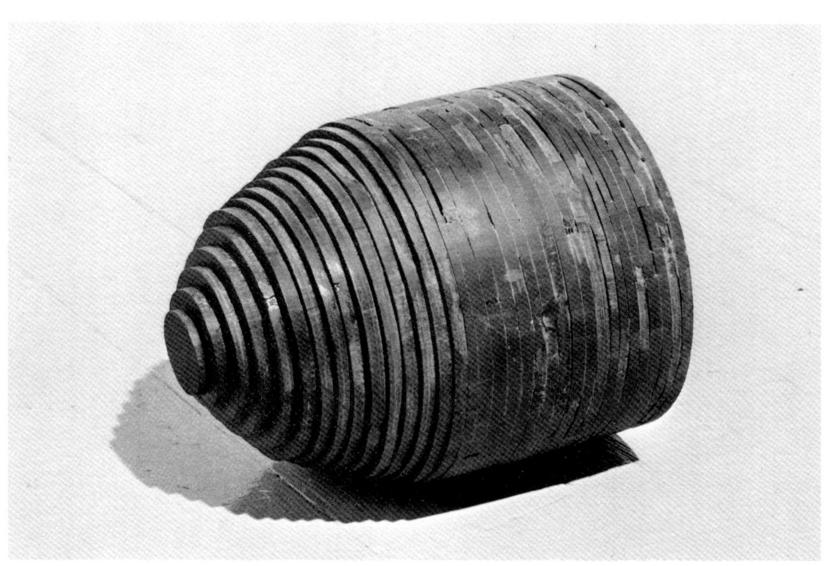

62 *Slate Projectile*, 1984
35 layers of laminated slate, 14 in. (h) x 12 in. (d)

objects are like words need not imply that they are signs with specific and interpretable referents. At the same time, the syntax construed by each grouping or installation of Lere's sculptures, as Structuralism suggests, accounts for their meaning.

63 *Parallax*, 1984
Metal blade, 32 x 100 x 18 in.

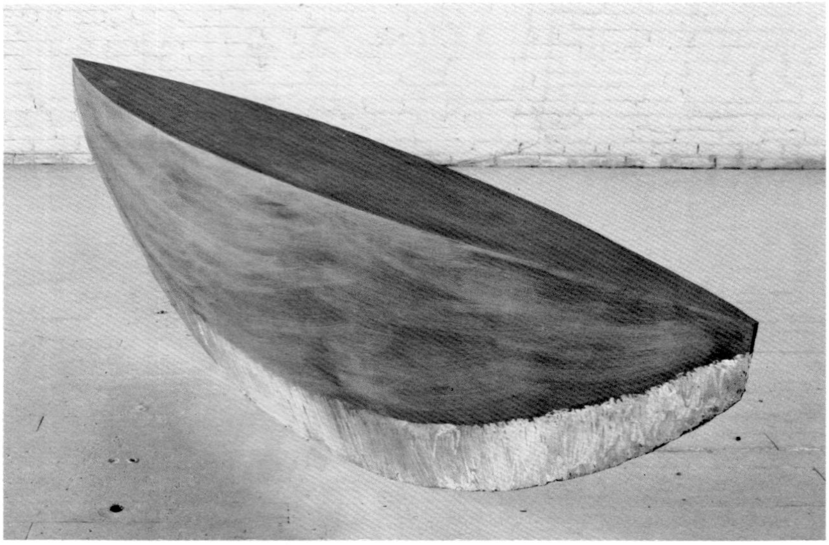

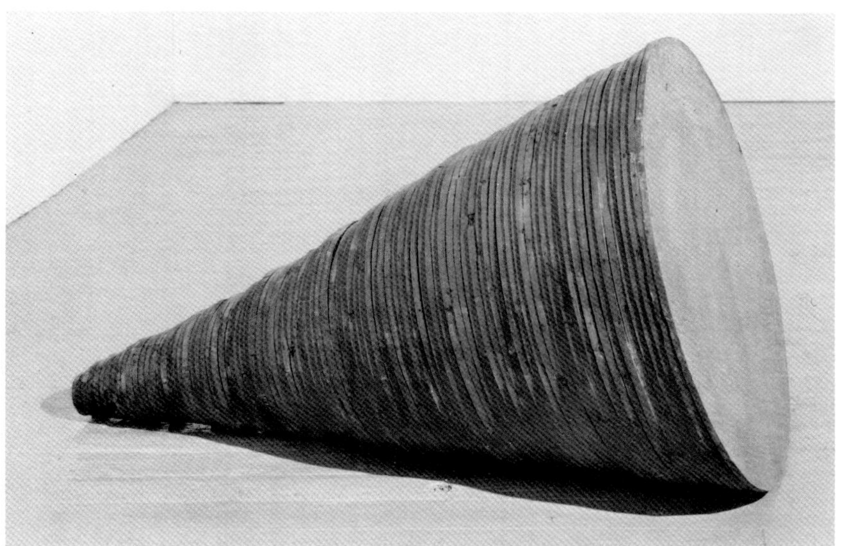

64 *Silence (Slate Megaphone)*, 1984
80 layers of laminated slate, 24 x 24 x 39 in.

¶ It cannot be said of Lere's sculp-

tures, as it can of sentences, that they

offer propositions of truth or false-

hood. He presents instead conceptual

gestures, as suggestions rather than

linguistic propositions capable of being

believed, doubted or denied. The same

delicacy of imagination characterizes

Lawrence Weiner's early *Statements.*

"One standard dye marker thrown into

the sea" and "One aerosol can of

enamel sprayed to conclusion directly

upon the floor" are not commands or

propositions but suggestions of graceful

gestures.

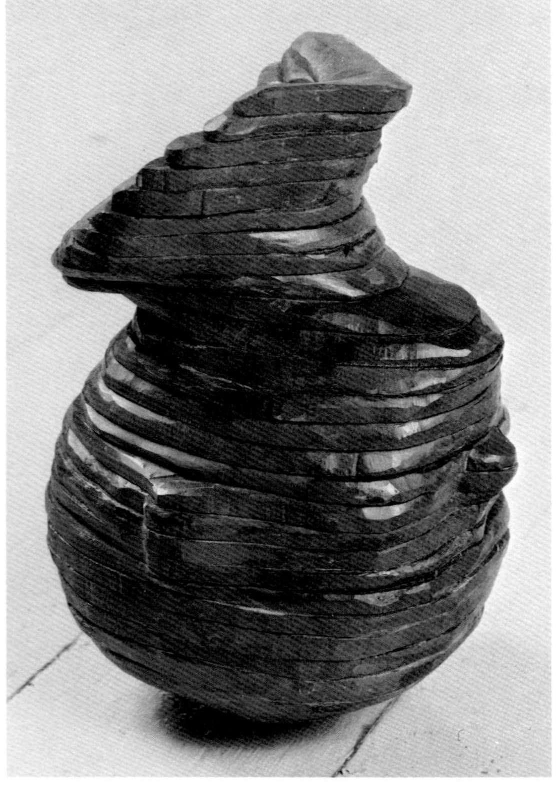

65 *Broca's Vessel*, 1984
Slate, 16 x 8 x 8 in.

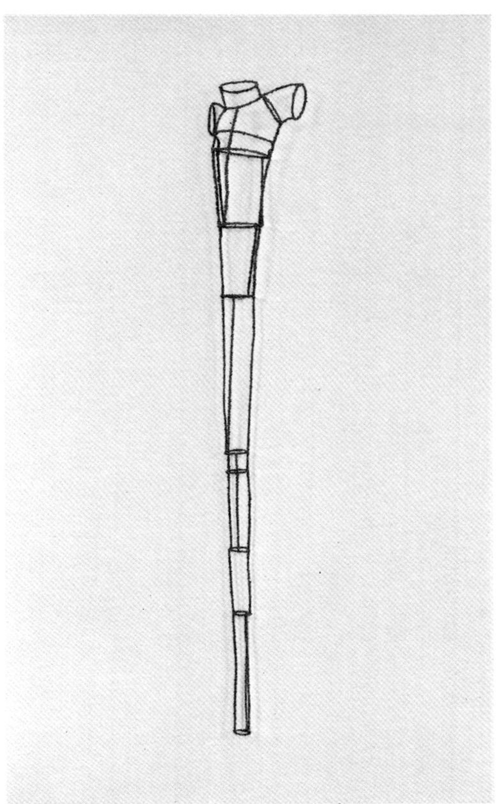

66 *Bronze Drawing*, 1984
Bronze, 86 x 12 x 6 in.

¶ **Lere discusses his own work in terms of "small gestures."** Lere's sculpture involves a process of transformation from the mundane to the magical, from the discursive to the poetic. Each small, potent gesture contributes to the metaphorical dialogue of his art.

I always figured in a sense that artists are displaced magicians. They're making these little gestures, these little objects, that somehow are going to influence something, either a person's thoughts or an action or even a physical thing. There's some fascination with the ability to do something small in a human sense. I think artists are the kind of people that are mystified by their own ability to make those small gestures.

1. Donald Judd, "Specific Objects," *Arts Yearbook 8* (New York: Art Digest, 1965), pp. 74-82. The specific object, as Judd used the term, is a work of art which is, in shape or form, single, indivisible and self-contained. It does not traffic in illusion but partakes of real space and identifiable materials. The term has entered art critical language and is now used primarily to refer to Minimal sculpture.

2. Statements by Mark Lere quoted throughout this essay are from "Notes on the 'Water Suites,'" *Water Suites* (Los Angeles: Municipal Art Gallery, 1983), n.p., and the author's interviews with the artist in 1984.

3. Bruce Nauman, unpublished interview with Lorraine Sciarra, quoted in Jane Livingston, *Bruce Nauman* (Los Angeles: Los Angeles County Museum of Art, 1972), p.22.

4. Lucy R. Lippard, "The Inside Picture from the Outside," in *Architectural Sculpture*, ed. Debra Burchett (Los Angeles: Los Angeles Institute of Contemporary Art, 1980), pp. 21-24.

5. Christina Lodder, *Russian Constructivism* (New Haven: Yale University Press, 1983), pp. 41-42.

6. Richard Artschwager, "The Hydraulic Doorcheck," *Arts Magazine*, vol. 42, no. 2 (November 1967), p. 41.

7. Michael Fried, "Art and Objecthood," *Artforum*, vol. 5, no. 10 (June 1967), pp. 19-22.

8. Donald B. Kuspit, "Authoritarian Abstraction," *Journal of Aesthetics and Art Criticism*, vol. 36, no. 1 (Fall 1977): 29; and "Authoritarian Aesthetics and The Elusive Alternative," *Journal of Aesthetics and Art Criticism*, vol. 41, no. 3 (Spring 1983), p. 280.

9. Jack Burnham, "Systems Esthetics," in *Great Western Salt-Works* (New York: Braziller, 1974), p. 17.

10. Julio Gonzalez, quoted in Rosalind Krauss, *Julio Gonzalez: Sculpture and Drawings* (New York: Pace Gallery, 1981), n.p.

11. Jack Burnham, "Hans Haacke—Wind and Water Sculpture," in *Art in the Land*, ed. Alan Sonfist (New York: E.P. Dutton, 1983), p. 118.

12. Robert Morris, "Notes on Sculpture, Part 2," *Artforum*, vol. 5, no. 2 (October 1966), p. 21.

13. F. David Martin, *Sculpture and Enlivened Space* (Lexington: University of Kentucky Press, 1981), pp. 133-34.

14. Robert Smithson, "Entropy and the New Monuments," *Artforum*, vol. 4, no. 10 (June 1966), p. 31.

15. Robert Morris, "Aligned with Nazca," *Artforum*, vol. 14, no. 1 (September 1975), p. 33.

16. Martin, *Sculpture and Enlivened Space*, pp. 89-90.

17. Philip Pettit, *The Concept of Structuralism: A Critical Analysis* (Berkeley: University of California Press, 1977), p. 62.

18. Jack Burnham, "The Purpose of the 'Ready-Mades,'" in *Great Western Salt-Works*, p. 74.

19. Ibid., p. 73.

20. Susanne K. Langer, *Feeling and Form: A Theory of Art* (New York: Charles Scribner's Sons, 1953), pp. 28-59 passim.

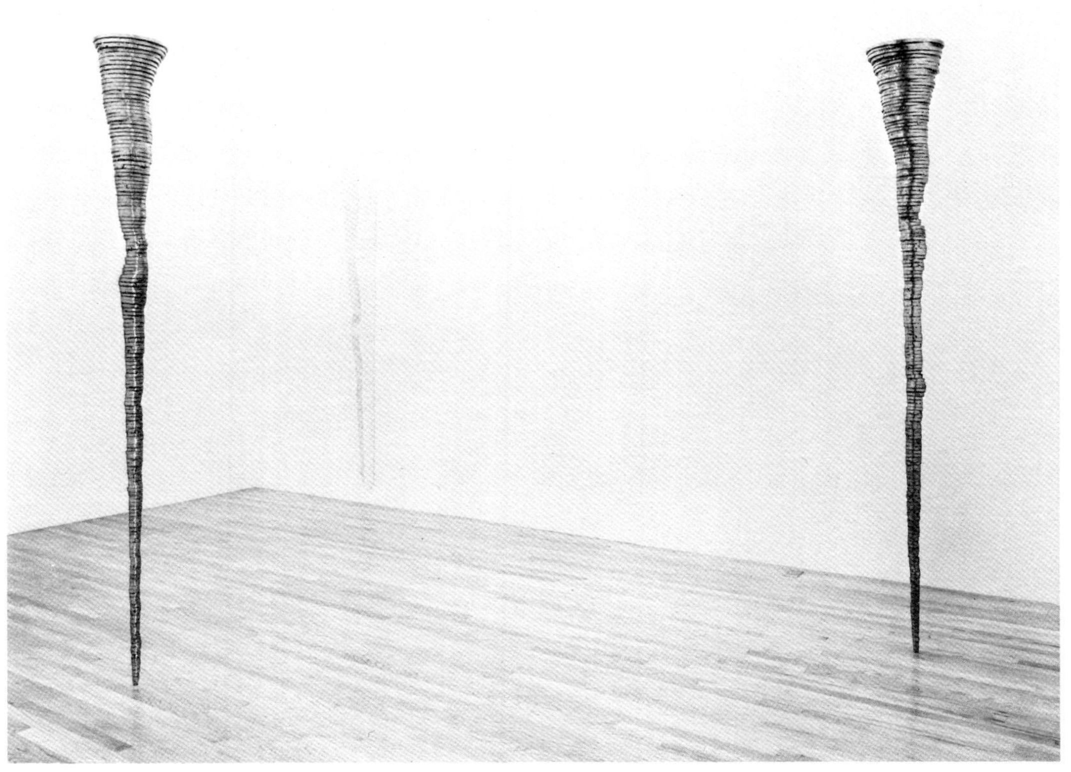

67 Installation, Riko Mizuno Gallery, 1983
Metal, 96 in. (h) x 12 in. (d); plaster, 92 x 12 x 6 in.

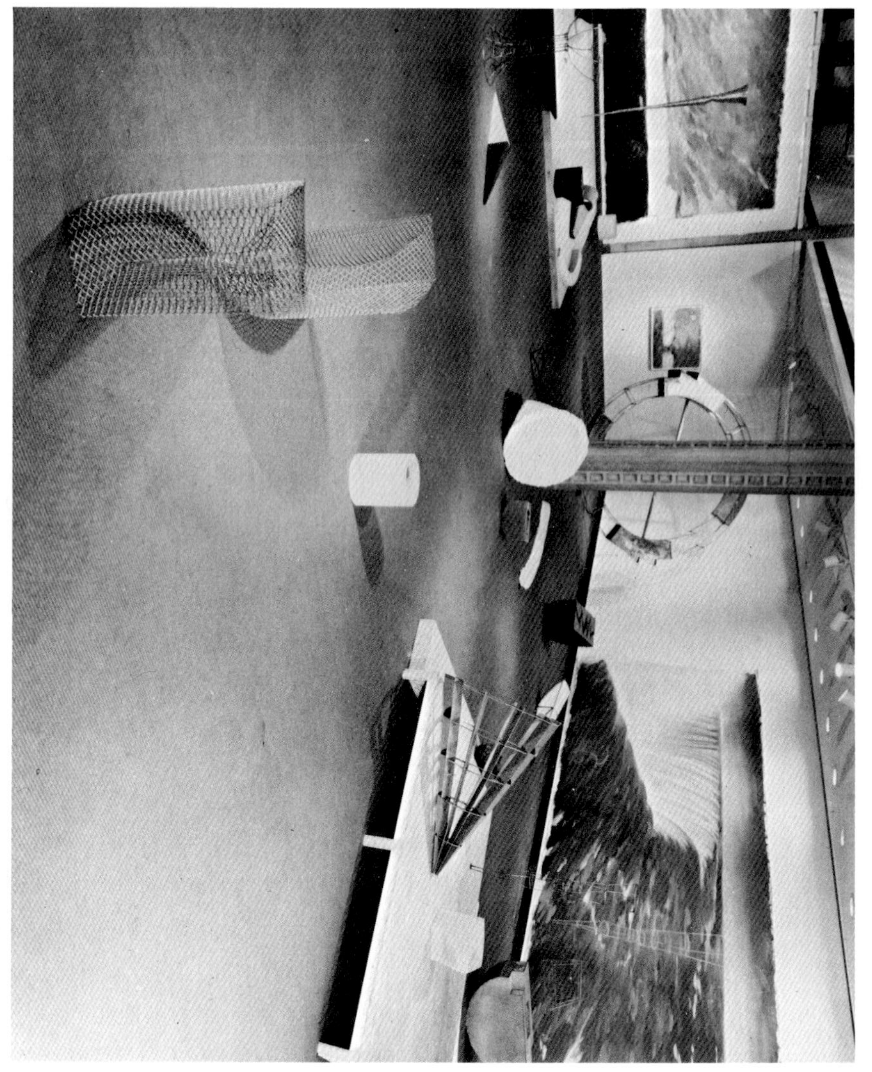

68, 69   *Water Suites*, 1984
Mixed media installation, Los Angeles
Municipal Art Gallery

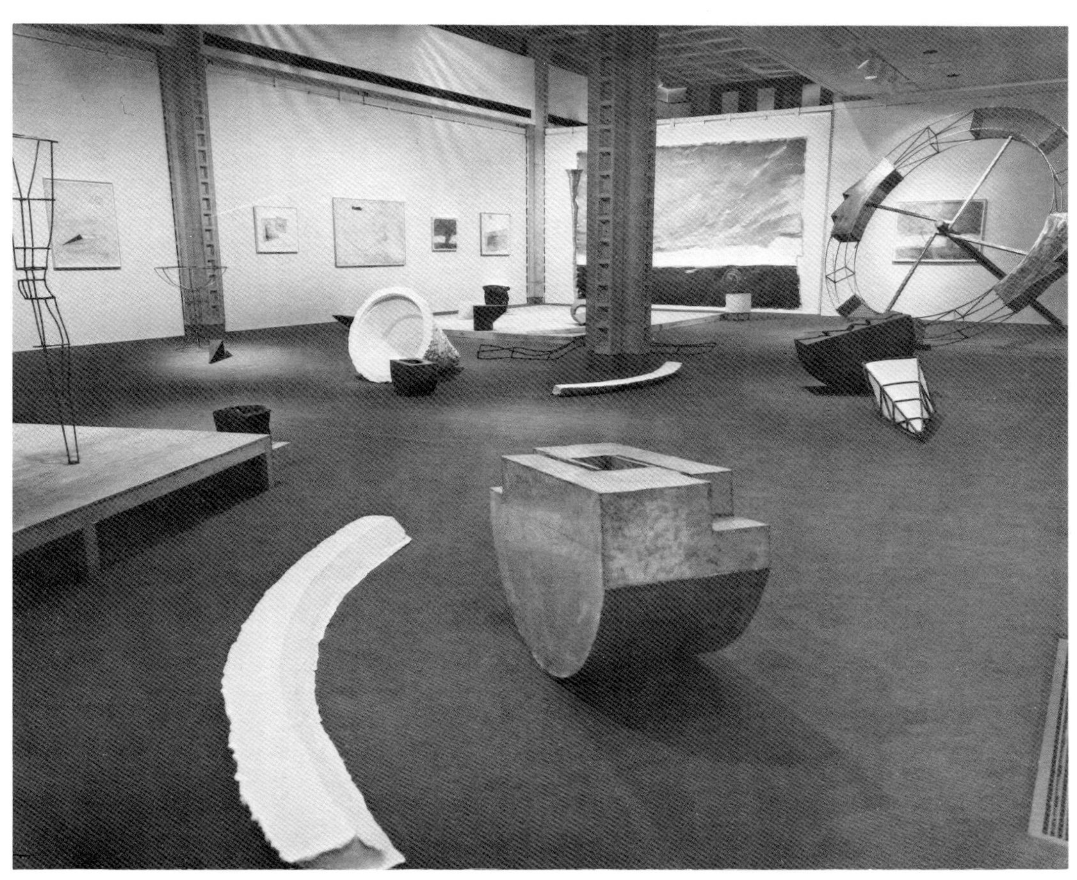

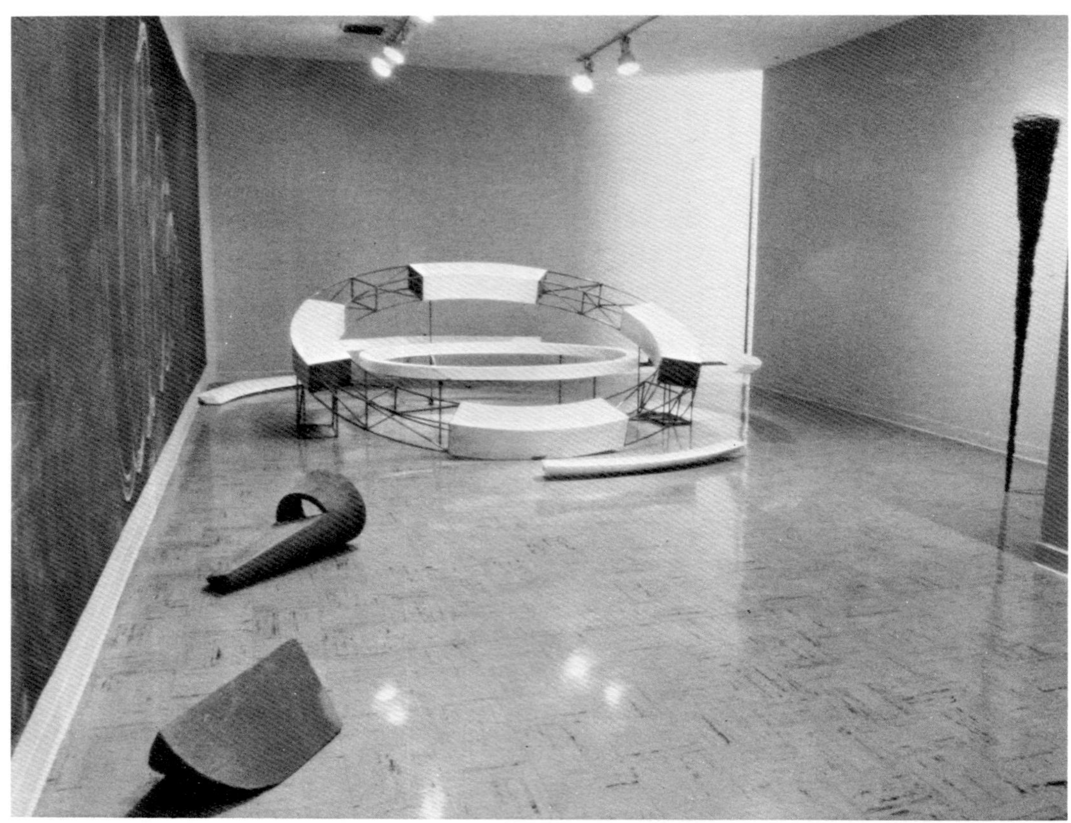

70 *Tornadoes Installation*, 1982
Mixed media installation, California State University,
Los Angeles

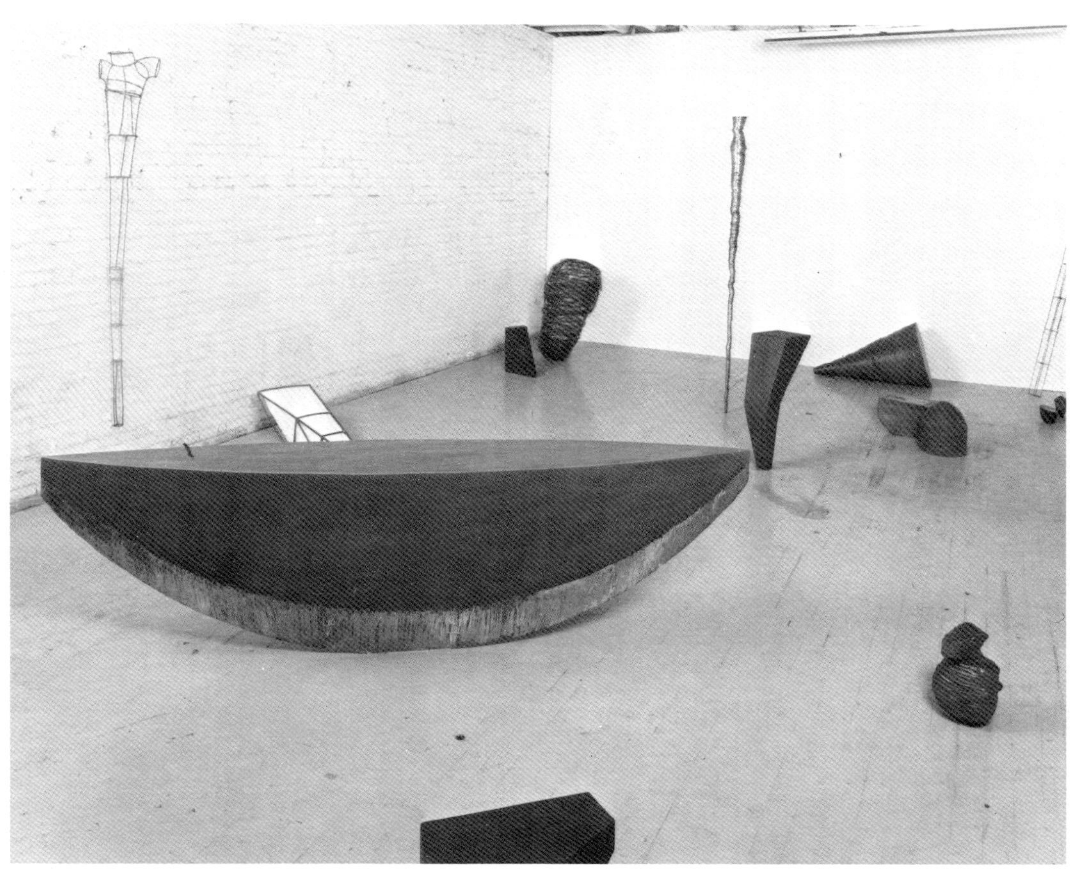

71 *Sympathetic Structures*, 1984
Mixed media studio installation

MARK LERE
HALO/WHEEL

Los Angeles, California

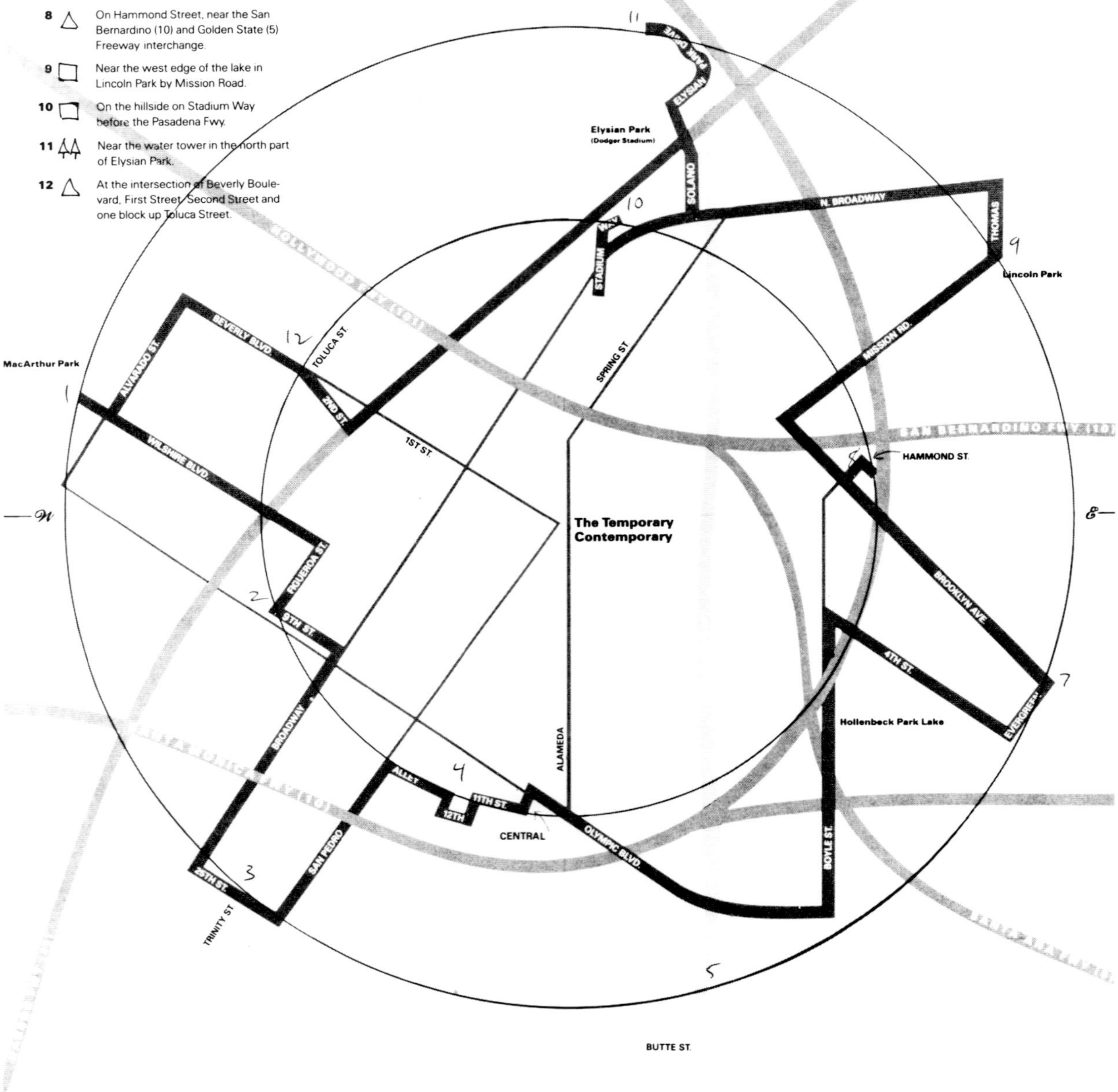

1 9 8 4

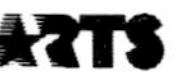

HALO/WHEEL

Kerry Brougher

61

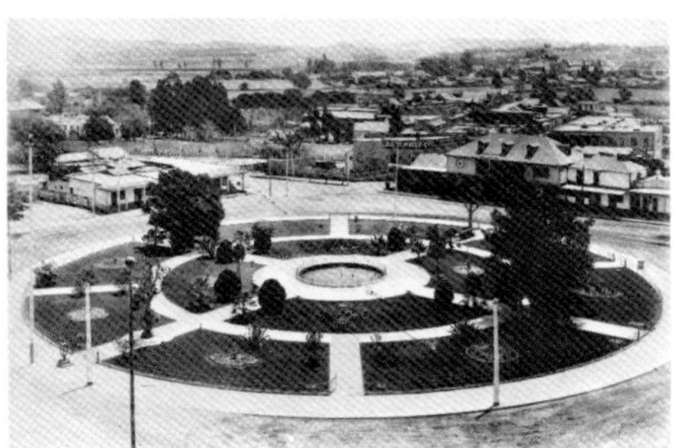

The City as Site and Sculpture

Mark Lere's *Halo/Wheel,* commissioned as a public exhibition by The Museum of Contemporary Art for the 1984 Olympic Arts Festival, was a work of art created out of the geographic experience of Los Angeles. The twelve-site piece, which was installed from July 21 through October 15, was the result of the forces and patterns at work in the city for which it was designed. As such it metaphorically offered a fresh view of the city's unique characteristics while simultaneously acting as a counterpoint to conventional ways of perceiving L.A., allowing the spectator to contemplate the city in new, unexpected and perhaps more appropriate terms.

¶ *Halo/Wheel* was designed for six park sites, five street locations and one area of the Los Angeles River. Each site was located on two imaginary concentric rings or wheels, the larger having a radius of 12,125 feet, that surrounded downtown Los Angeles with the Museum's Temporary Contemporary at the center. Each work was a fragment of the large conceptual ring on which it lay, echoing its arc and using materials appropriate to that location. Most of the works were comprised of painted elements or cast sculptural forms. The street locations, for example, consisted of shapes painted directly on the road. These elements followed the arc of one of the large imaginary circles as it cut across streets and intersections, disappeared into a curb or building and picked up again on the other side of a block or

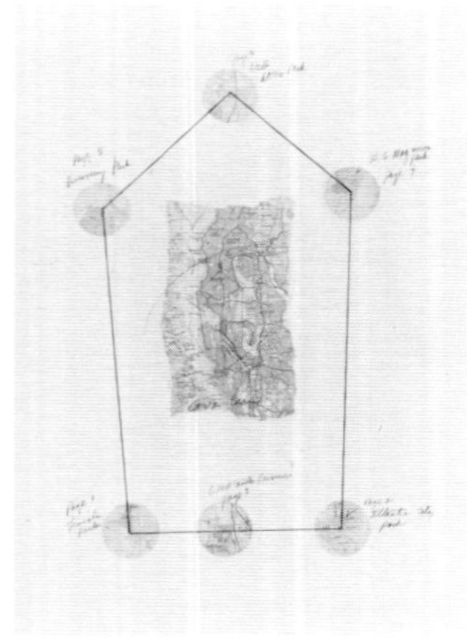

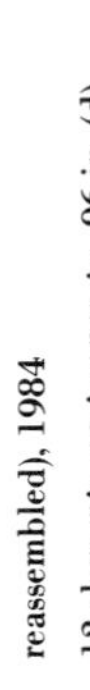

72 Drawing for *Seattle Scatter*, 1980
Graphite on Herculene, 30 x 20 in.

73, 74 *Halo/Wheel* (MacArthur Park site elements reassembled), 1984
12 elements, cast concrete, 96 in. (d)

alley. Four of the six park sites (MacArthur, Elysian near Stadium Way, Lincoln and Trinity) were composed of sculptural elements. MacArthur Park, for instance, contained a large concrete wheel that had been fragmented into twelve individual wedges, which also were distributed along the path of the circle that sliced through this location.

¶ *Halo/Wheel* operated on a number of levels. Referring to the map with its legend for the kinds of pieces (painted element, floating element, etc.), one could use the clues to find the often discreet works of art, thus inhabiting the work as a whole and searching out its secrets and treasures in much the same way one would in an unfamiliar city. This multi-site format developed out of *Seattle Scatter,* a work currently under construction, in which Lere proposes to install houseboat-shaped elements at five sites that also form a houseboat outline when linked on a map.

¶ Just as most Angelenos never venture into all the exotic and far-flung locales of their city, one did not need to experience every site of *Halo/Wheel* to comprehend the work as a whole. The concept for the piece was as central to its purpose as the individual works themselves. It was the two-dimensional, map-like origins of the piece which were the important mode of approaching the work. L.A. itself is probably better known by its citizens through their maps than by physical experience; if one needs to get to the other side of town, the freeway map is consulted, and the trek is made without much fuss

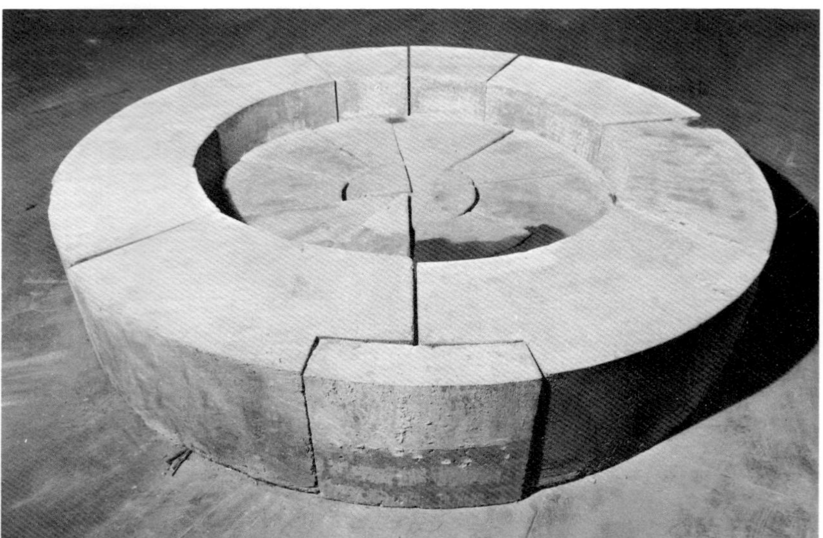

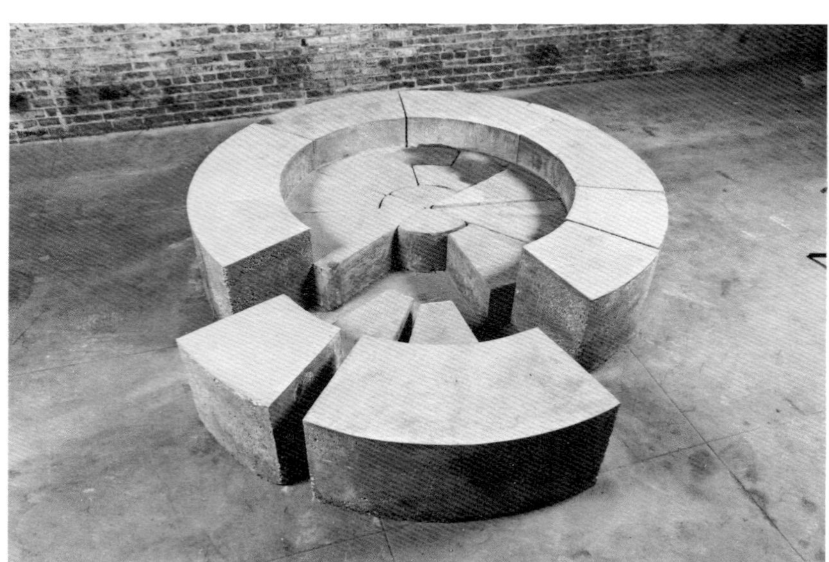

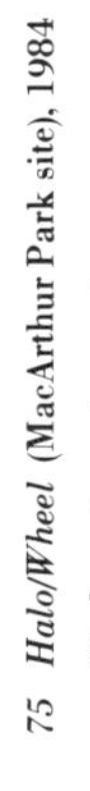

75 *Halo/Wheel* (MacArthur Park site), 1984
12 elements, cast concrete

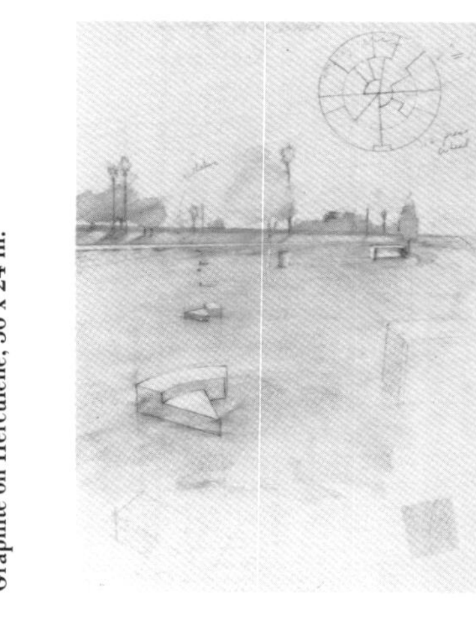

76 Drawing for *Halo/Wheel* (MacArthur Park site), 1984
Graphite on Herculene, 36 x 24 in.

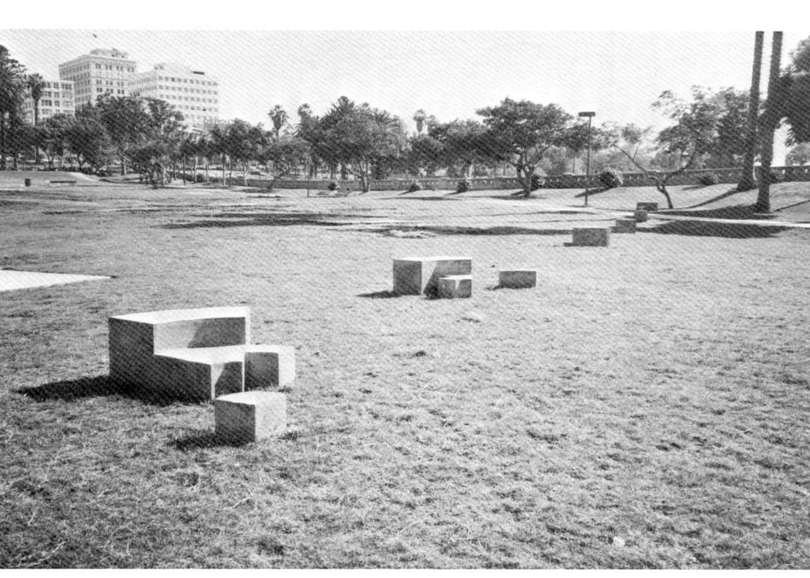

and with little understanding of what is passed through to get there. Always interested in the symbolism of surveying and cartology and the ways in which people come to know their territories vicariously through linear guides, Lere created a conceptual work that functioned in a similar manner. He outlined the structure thoroughly on paper in the hope that upon visiting one or two sites, the traveler would come to understand his location in relation to the other sites, to comprehend the spaces that lay between and obtain a general idea of the nature of each work in relation to the whole. ¶ To fully grasp *Halo/Wheel*, however, one must consider the way Lere extracted the piece from its host city and the manner in which the work converged with that city. *Halo/Wheel* was not a work of art laid over an area; rather, it grew naturally out of both the physical and psychological superstructure of Los Angeles. ¶ The framework of the piece was the two imaginary concentric rings, which were emblematic of the City of Angels and the important role the automobile has played in its development. These circles also reiterated Lere's interest in elliptical orbits and the drainage of liquids apparent in his series of circular constructions of 1980-83. Originally intending to fix the center of *Halo/ Wheel* at the point of the city's origin, Lere soon discovered that no one really knew exactly where the original Pueblo of Los Angeles had been located, as a result of its having been moved numerous times due to floods and earthquakes.[1] Lere then decided to center

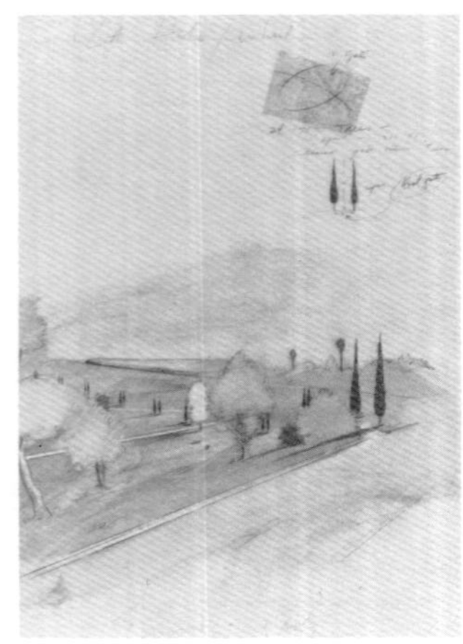

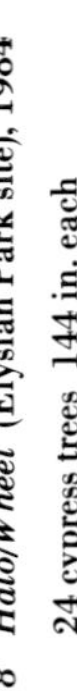

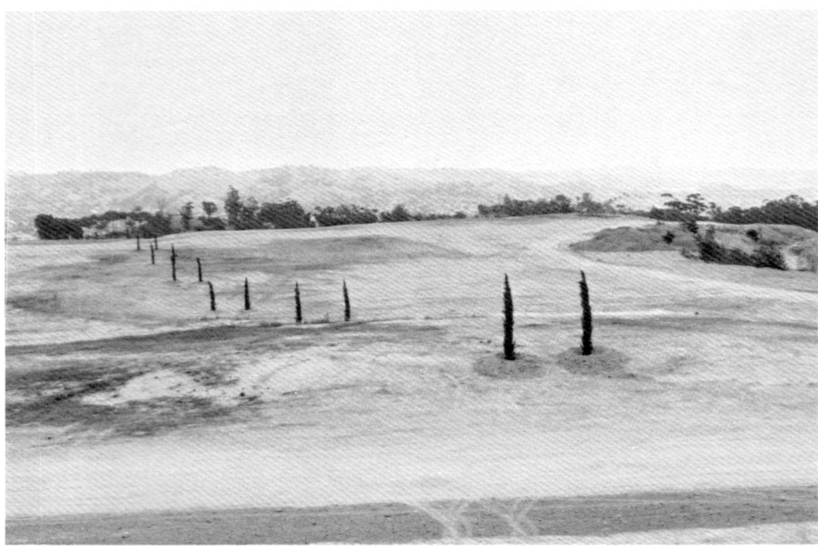

the work at MOCA's Temporary Contemporary, located near the Olvera Street complex that historians believe is close to the original Pueblo. Having fixed the center, Lere adjusted the rings to cover diverse areas of downtown Los Angeles. He drew radii until each circle was intersected six times, creating twelve distinct points. Located across from one another on their respective halos, these points became the locations for the actual site pieces to be installed. In researching the work, Lere found a photo of the original plaza in the 1870s which, to his surprise, showed two concentric rings linked by radiating walkways.

¶ The sites were not firmly fixed until the artist had visited each one several times, exploring various possibilities for form and materials. Changes were made: some locations did not lend themselves well to the theme of the arc, others seemed to lack the variety required by Lere and still others proved impossible because of the restrictions of property owners. The process was not one of forcing the arc on the site nor was it an attempt to locate existing curves or tangents that would easily receive the concept of the halo. Rather, to create the necessary sense of enlightenment about the space in the visitor, it was necessary to play the arc off of, but not to fight with, the geographic configuration.

¶ The materials varied greatly throughout the piece and were chosen for their appropriateness to each location. Like Lere's previous work, the three-dimensional pieces used such construction materials as concrete, steel and ply-

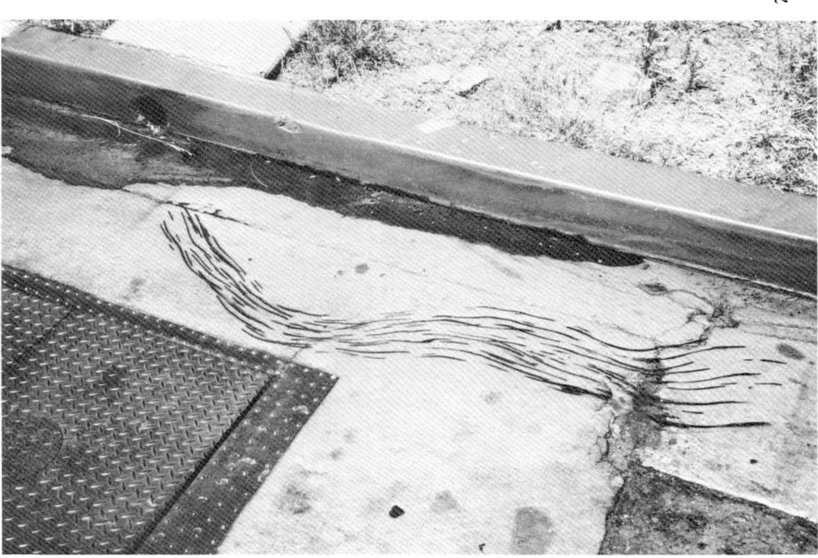

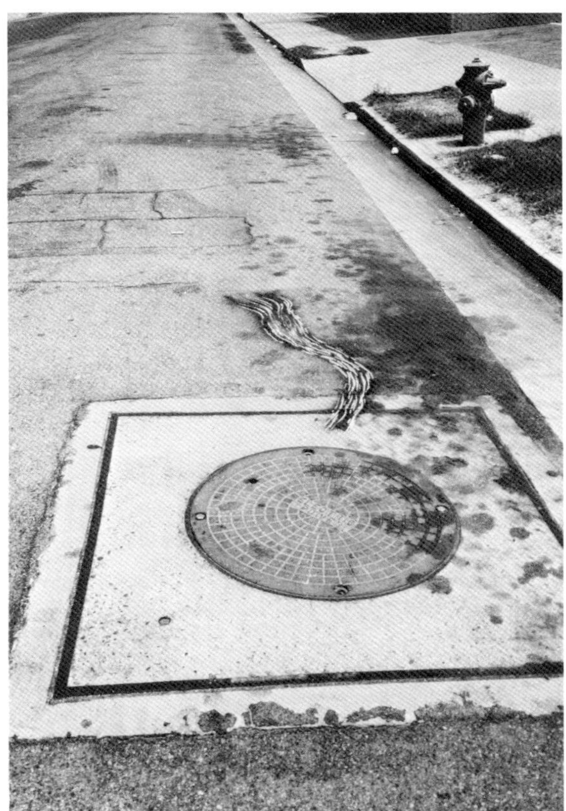

wood, which seemed to be reflective of the tough, durable, practical aspects of the city itself. However, other sites dictated more natural media. One was Elysian Park, where Lere planted twenty-four Italian cypress trees in rows of two's, following the arc and setting up an association with the tree-lined roads of Europe and, in turn, the real highways used at other locations of *Halo/Wheel*. The street works, on the other hand, found their inspiration in the two-dimensional symbolism of the road; paint became the medium to denote Lere's personal imagery of stairways, prosthetics and the flow of water. This countered the flat, two-dimensional appearance of the street and inspired such questions as "What lies beneath the road and under manhole covers?"

¶ Although most public sculpture attempts to take into account the general environment and specific setting, the result, nevertheless, often appears to be an intrusion into a space that was never meant to contain sculpture. Lere avoided this with his ever-present attempt to raise the piece organically, not only out of the site but also out of the psychological and aesthetic sensibilities of the local inhabitants and city officials. Rather than approach municipal personnel with a fully developed, formidable proposal, Lere began the process of obtaining city permits for his installations while the piece was still forming in his own mind, thus providing ample room for the work to be shaped or slightly restructured by forces that were more or less out of the artist's control. Thus, a very

important link was formed between the work and the mental pulse of the city into which it nestled. As Lere himself admits, in both *Halo/Wheel* and *Seattle Scatter*, this process produced suggestions and stumbling blocks that led to a rethinking of several site works and, eventually, to solutions that he felt were even better suited to the site and the nature of the work as a whole.
¶ Lere's ongoing "Water Suite" series utilizes a vocabulary of diverse water-related forms and the natural and mythic associations inherent in each of those forms that, when juxtaposed, create something akin to "a musical suite where one element or instrument brings diverse units together in a composition."[2] *Halo/Wheel* also became a complex composition, a huge jig-saw puzzle to be organized in the mind in much the same way as Los Angeles with its diverse ecologies and varied blanket of communities must be conceived to form a picture of the whole. The sites and their respective works commented on one another in the same manner as the communities of L.A.: one cannot appreciate either Beverly Hills or East Los Angeles without experiencing both as well as other areas of the city. Likewise, one could not fully assimilate the meaning of the concrete fragments Lere installed in MacArthur Park without also taking into consideration the variety of ways in which he integrated sculpture or painting with the conceptual arcs elsewhere. Though each site was in some sense an independent element, one became aware of its role in the organizational pattern of the whole, and it was impossible to know

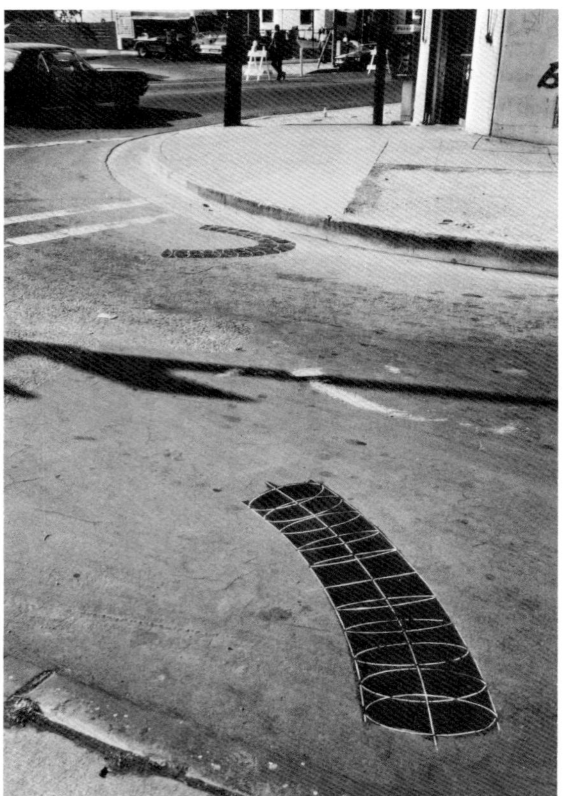

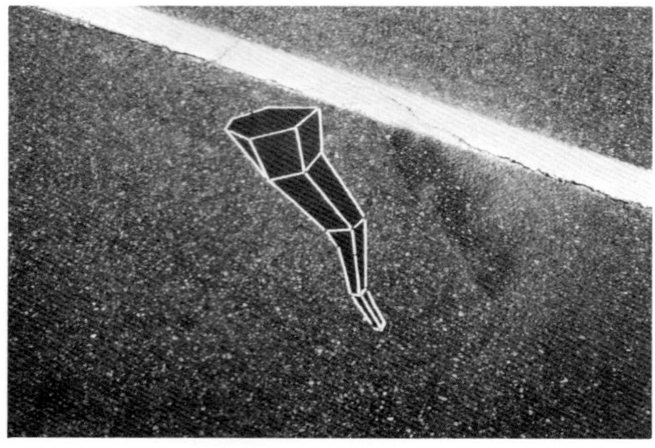

82 *Halo/Wheel* (9th and Figueroa Streets site), 1984
12 elements, enamel on asphalt

84 *Halo/Wheel* (Hammond Street site), 1984
12 elements, enamel on asphalt

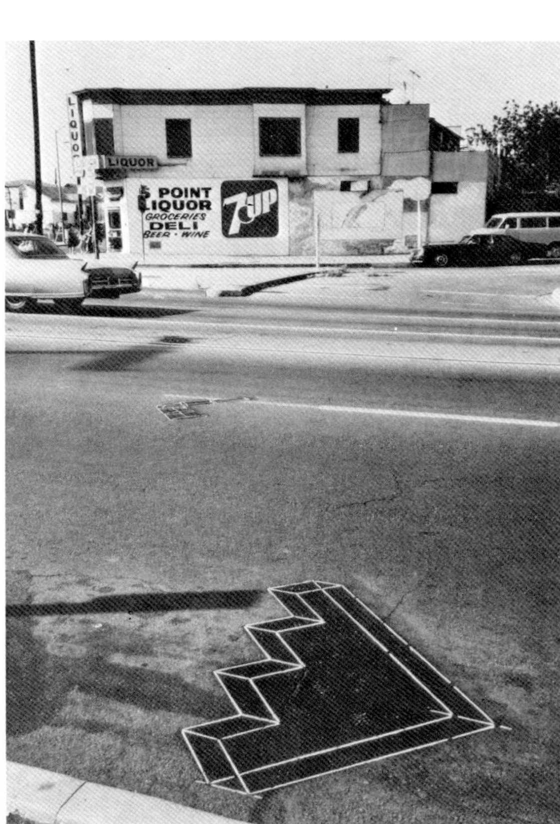

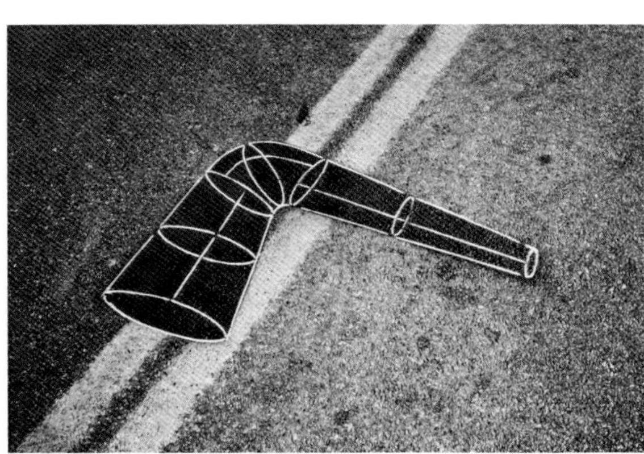

the whole without some understanding of its parts.

¶ In much of his previous work, particularly the "Water Suites," Lere has attempted to control and analyze movement in nature and the implied associations relevant to the cause of such movement. *Halo/Wheel* worked in a similar manner, capturing the centrifugal flow of L.A. outward from the vortex of the original Pueblo and forcing the viewer to rotate from one site to the next. To experience the piece, one had to drive and expend time, and this act of motion, which required the physical participation of the audience, became an essential ingredient of the work. As one moved around the circles, the sights and sounds of L.A. became more apparent, more tangible; the busy streets, crowded neighborhoods, vacant lots and last remnants of wilderness began to take on an unexpected reality. The auto ceased to be a small, autonomous spaceship hurtling rapidly through the confines of freeway corridors and became, rather, a tool for exploration. The biproduct of this spacio-temporal and kinetic experience was a better understanding of Angelenos' sense of freedom through mobility; the city's transportation network was used for a fresh confrontation with the everyday.

¶ *Halo/Wheel* also showed evidence of Lere's continuing interest in creating a dialogue between such opposites as positive and negative, shape and line, two dimensions and three dimensions. Restricting the location of the sites to opposite "sides" of the circles, Lere put emphasis on the viewer's need to relate

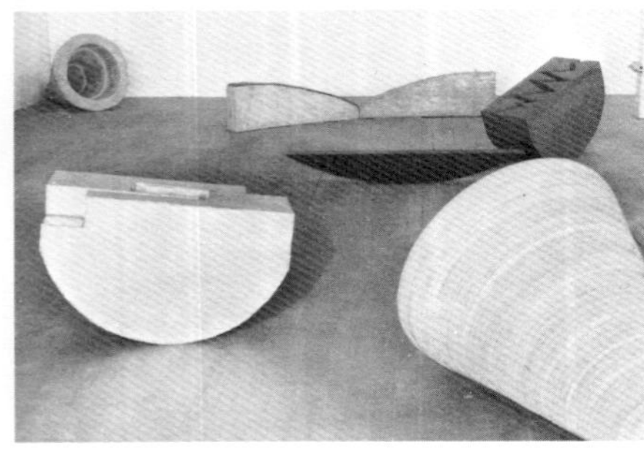

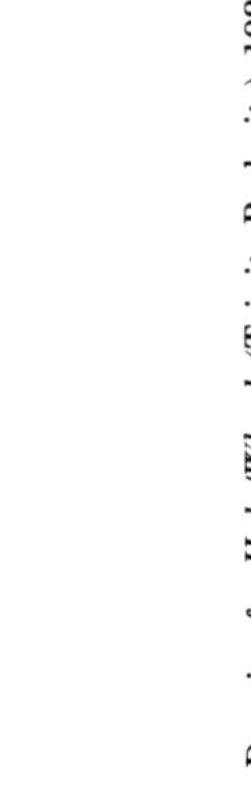

85 *Water Suites, Act I*, 1981
Mixed media installation in artist's studio

86 *Halo/Wheel* (Trinity Park site), 1984
12 elements, cast concrete

87 Drawing for *Halo/Wheel* (Trinity Park site), 1984
Graphite on Herculene, 36 x 24 in.

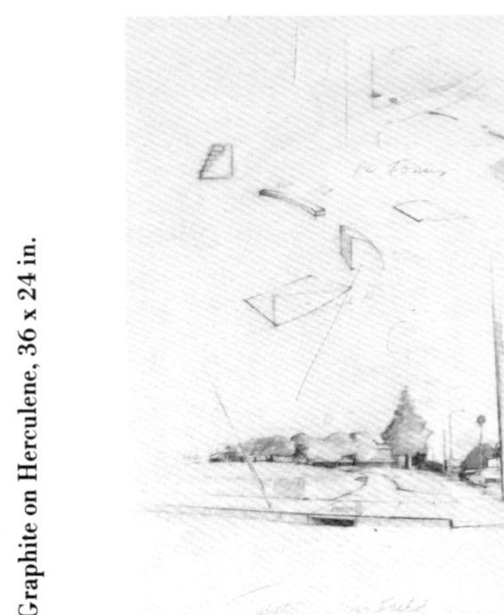

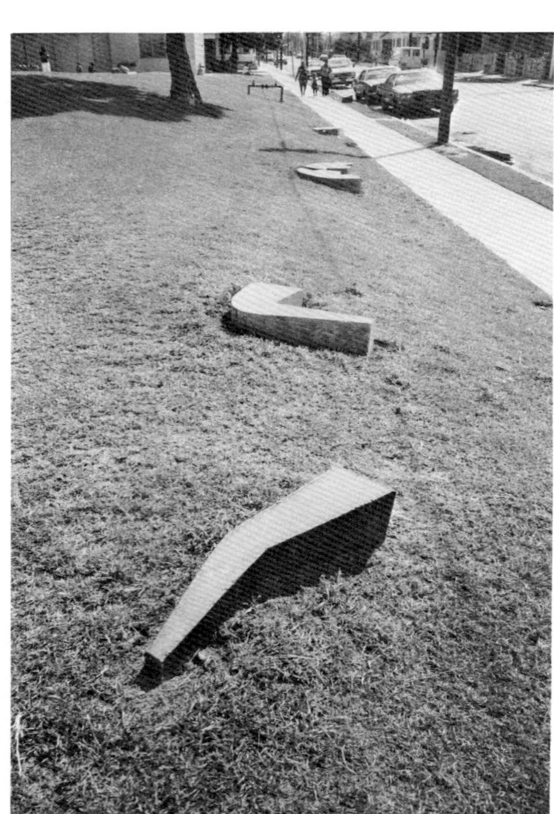

to other appropriate points in L.A. that were not connected by the visual and psychological aid of a street or freeway. The audience had to make a mental leap across town and in so doing came to perceive the downtown area as something more than a grid of streets, parking lots and buildings. Spaces were defined by distance, scale, shape and their relationship to one another rather than by their location as a series of points on a transportation artery.

¶ Shape and line relationships also entered into the design. Most of the park pieces were three-dimensional concrete or metal shapes, but because they were only parts of a larger wheel and that wheel only a point on a larger, more "powerful" circle, the artist denied them the force and presence generally associated with sculpture. Instead, they remained fragments that had to be read in linear fashion in order to fit the pieces back together. To accommodate this process, Lere often kept the forms flat and weighty as if they were sprouting from the earth rather than lying on it. Indeed, Lincoln Park's metal arcs were literally implanted into the ground, creating a clean, linear, two-dimensional work that perhaps related more to technical drawings, road symbols and maps than to sculpture.

¶ Negative and positive coexisted in Lere's work. Splitting the circle into many sites—and often the site work into many individual elements with space in between—echoed Lere's method of drawing, in which he erases through positive lines and shapes, thus

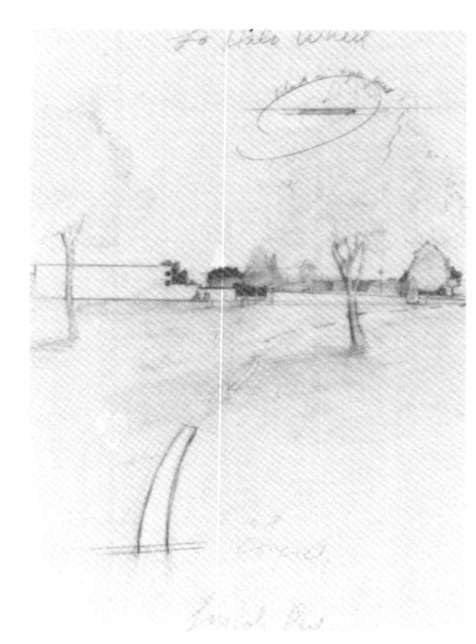

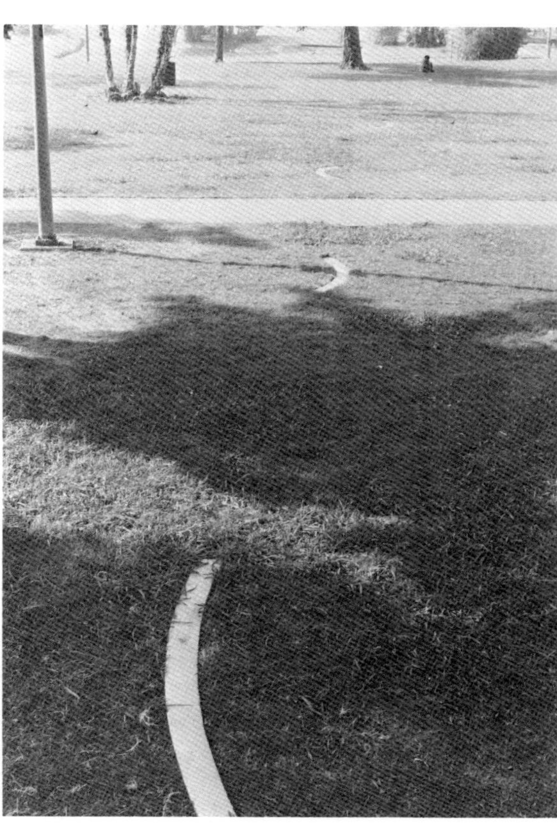

88 *Halo/Wheel* (Lincoln Park site), 1984
12 elements, cast concrete

89 Drawing for *Halo/Wheel* (Lincoln Park site, final version), 1984
Graphite on Herculene, 36 x 24 in.

forcing the spectator to complete the picture. The artist went a step further in Elysian Park near Stadium Way, creating a piece that resembled his previous *Drains* and wall depressions. He cut a "bench" into a side of a hill, thus forming a negative space, the void taking on the characteristics of a functional, positive space. One could look out over the downtown area and the other sites and contemplate the work as an entire unit, almost as if one were reading a map. The line between reality and symbol here again became blurred.

¶ The theme and image of water, which has recurred throughout Lere's work, cropped up in *Halo/Wheel*, and rightly so, since water, or the lack of it, has been an important factor in L.A.'s development. At Hollenbeck Park, a large wooden ellipse floated in the man-made lake, reflecting its shape like a dark, negative halo on the bottom of the Golden State Freeway overpass. The river site depended on the absence of water and used the river bed and walls as the surface for a painted ellipse that linked the west and east banks. The fact that little or no water runs through the channel during summer and fall—the duration of the exhibition—was, of course, essential to the realization of the piece and recalled Lere's drains and fountains that outline the shape of water but do not make use of the actual substance. As in his previous work, Lere remained sensitive to other natural elements as well. If he forged L.A. into an idealistic, perfect circle, it was not one untouched by cataclysm.

The works at MacArthur and Trinity
parks and Lere's drawing for the
exhibition poster, with their shattered,
cracked wedge shapes, took into account the forces of nature that often
reek havoc on this city: earthquakes,
floods, fires and drought. This was
certainly no carefully divided pie but a
utopia split apart arbitrarily and often
violently by nature.

¶ The flatness, diversity and scale of
Halo/Wheel found their origin in the
explosion of suburbia that surrounds
Los Angeles, a logical extension of the
city's skeletal framework—the railroad.
By the 1880s, the lines of the Southern
Pacific had established an exceedingly
efficient way of moving goods and
people over vast distances relatively
quickly, allowing settlers the benefit of
living in a rural environment while
remaining close enough to the city to
carry on their business transactions.
These same transportation routes later
defined the paths of the major freeways, thus providing for further ex-
pansion outward.[3] Lere's *Halo/Wheel*
also revolved around a center focus
and radiated out from it, forming satel-
lite sites (read communities) on the
fringes of its inner space. Over the
years, the actual downtown core of Los
Angeles had the life sucked out of it
by its offspring but remained, even
before the recent redevelopment, as the
structural hub of a vast, mobile wheel.
The heart of *Halo/Wheel* was also
essentially a void but one—like the eye
of a hurricane—from which energy
emanated.

¶ The often-discussed flat expanses
of L.A. also concerned Lere in his

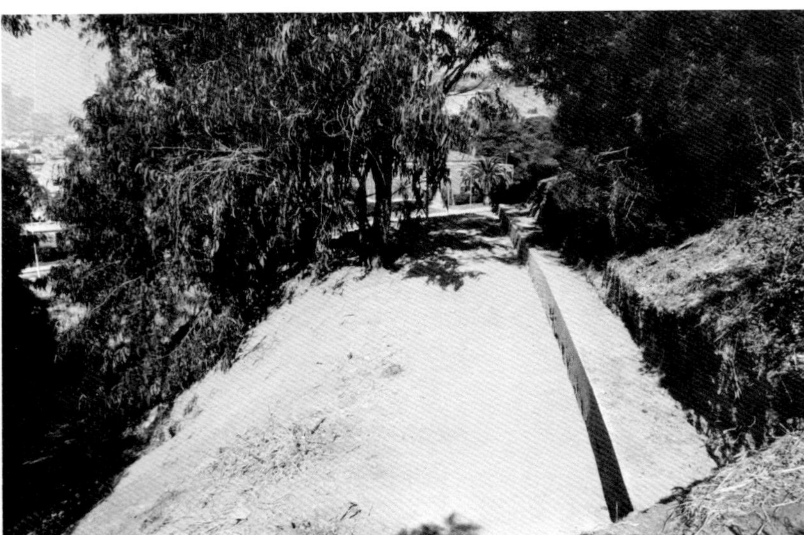

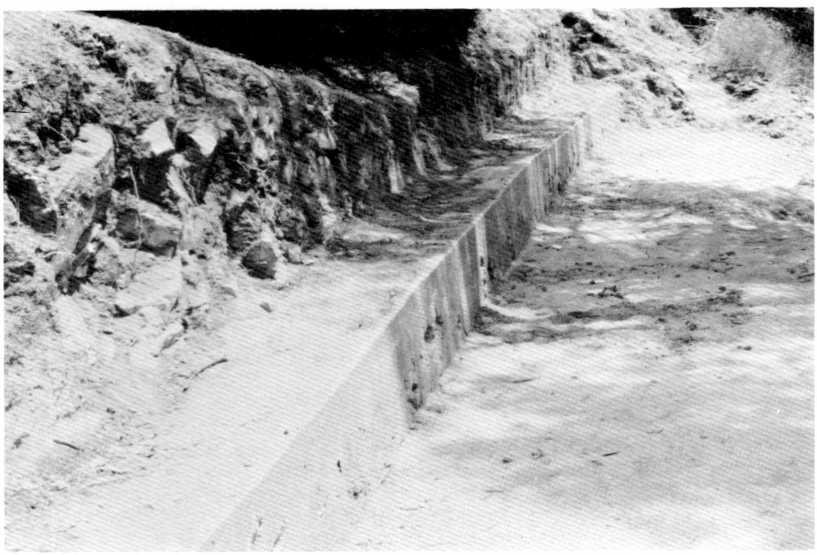

92 *Halo/Wheel* (Trinity Park site), 1984
12 elements, cast concrete

93 Drawing for *County Line Neon*, 1970
Graphite on Herculene, 24 x 12 in.

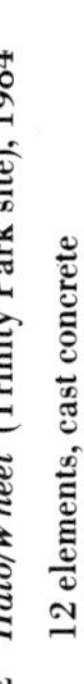

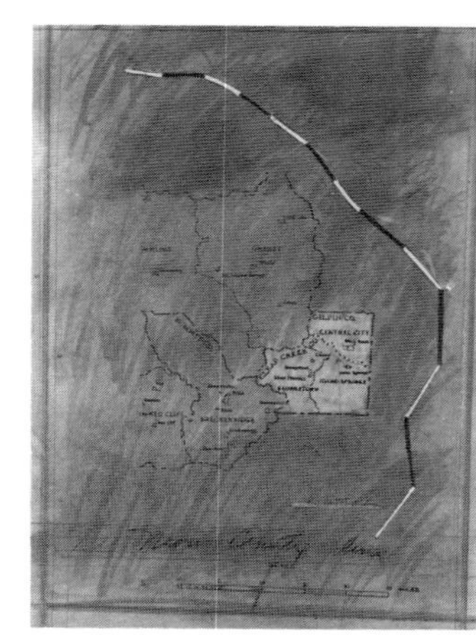

integration of sculptural volume with two-dimensional painting and drawing. *Halo/Wheel* was essentially a flat, two-dimensional work; some sites were actually painted—not on a wall but right on the street—while the sites that were sculptural seemed to hide their volume through their low-lying features and the fact that they were placed on the conceptual line of the circle, which in itself had no dimension. When Lere did venture into plasticity, he did so without fanfare or monumentality. The cypress trees in Elysian Park were denied their stature by an environment that received them naturally and quietly. This dialectic between the monumental and the discreet was most certainly a result of Los Angeles's own grandeur, which can be viewed only from the air, not from the ground. The city is an endless expanse only when seen from a plane or on a map; in that sense, Los Angeles does indeed remain a two-dimensional place, perhaps more real on the map than in actuality.

¶ This ambiguous relationship between reality and the symbolism of maps has interested Lere since his student days in Denver. In 1970, while attending Metropolitan State College, Lere reproduced a county line by laying down tubes of neon on the land, focusing the viewer's attention on the arbitrariness of such symbolism. In *Halo/Wheel*, Lere sliced right through intersections, parks and freeways with his concentric circles, again drawing our attention to these separations and the inherent limitations that radiate out with almost iconographic power from the two-

dimensional surface of a map. Even
such natural barriers as hillsides or
rivers, which often resist manipulation
of any sort, became integral parts of
Halo/Wheel. The cumulative result was
that our normal perception of the
urban configuration as landmarks,
barriers and borders with their restric-
tive overtones was tempered and soft-
ened. The L.A. River, for example, with
its psychological connotation of a wall
between East Los Angeles and the rest
of the city, reverted through Lere's
work of art to its real function as a
natural barrier, nothing more.
¶ *Halo/Wheel* no longer exists as a
whole. The constructed and sculpted
pieces have been dismantled and will
no doubt be recycled, as is the artist's
habit, into other works; the painted
pieces are slowly being ground into the
asphalt, fading into the surface of the
city. But the subject of the work remains: an entire city including the connotations and the associations each
viewer carries with him. Unlike *Seattle
Scatter*, in which each site will retain a
certain integrity as an art object, many
works of *Halo/Wheel* were little more
than signposts, revealing some aspect
of Los Angeles and reminding the
viewer of the configuration of the
entire project, which in turn alluded to
the larger organism of the city. Lere's
long interest in referential forms was
still apparent, but *Halo/Wheel* did not
rely on metaphor alone. If it was Lere's
intention to use the city to form the
piece and thus to reveal the city
through the work, it was also his desire
to use the urban environment as part
of the raw material, both in terms of

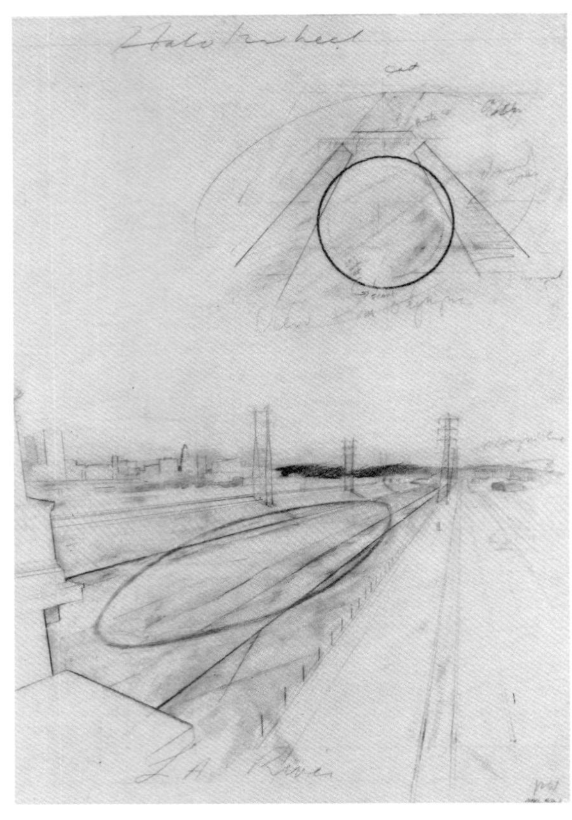

94 Drawing for *Halo/Wheel* (Los Angeles River site), 1984
Pencil on Herculene, 36 x 24 in.

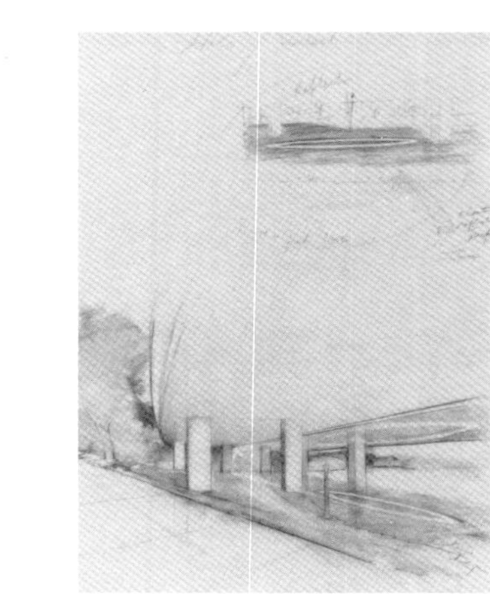

95 *Halo/Wheel* (Hollenbeck Park site), 1984
Floating wood elements, 6 x 48 x 1480 in.

96 Drawing for *Halo/Wheel* Hollenbeck Park site), 1984
Pencil on Herculene, 36 x 24 in.

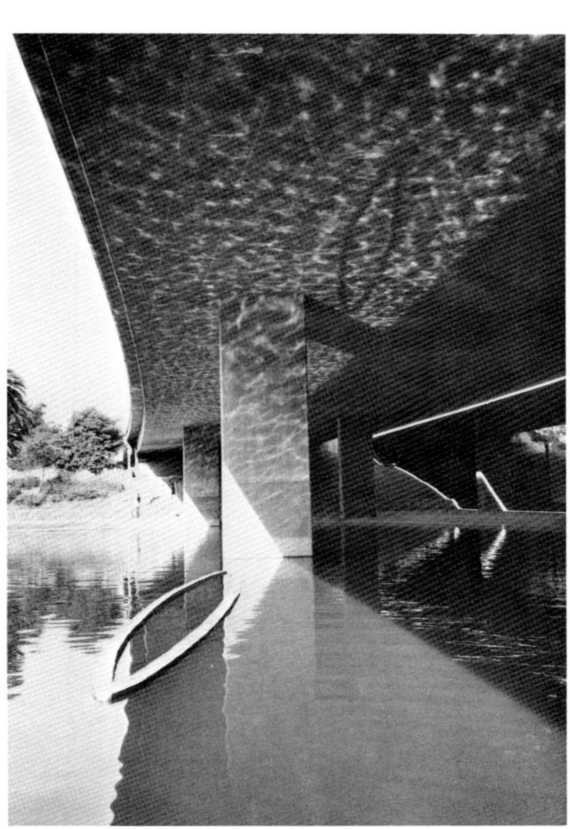

each site and for the journey between sites. Los Angeles, then, was both the subject and at times the medium of the piece, and the visitor a conduit between the two. Los Angeles became more identifiable and the visitor more integrated with his environment.

1. Reyner Banham, *Los Angeles: The Architecture of Four Ecologies* (New York: Harper & Row, 1971), p. 207.

2. Mark Lere, "Notes on the *'Water Suites'*," (Los Angeles: Municipal Art Gallery, 1983), n.p.

3. Banham, *Los Angeles*, pp. 75-77.

S Los Angeles, 1981

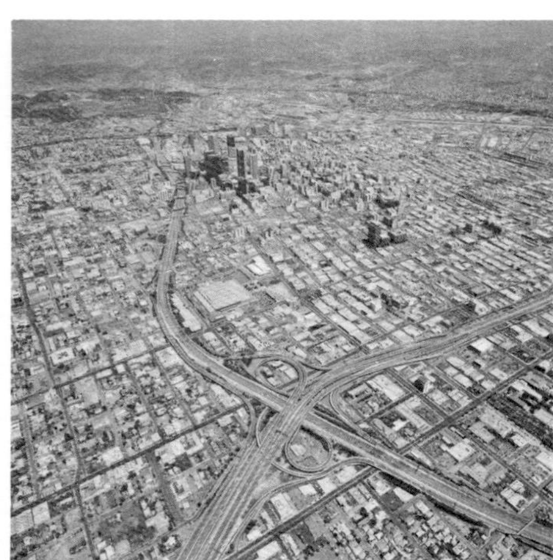

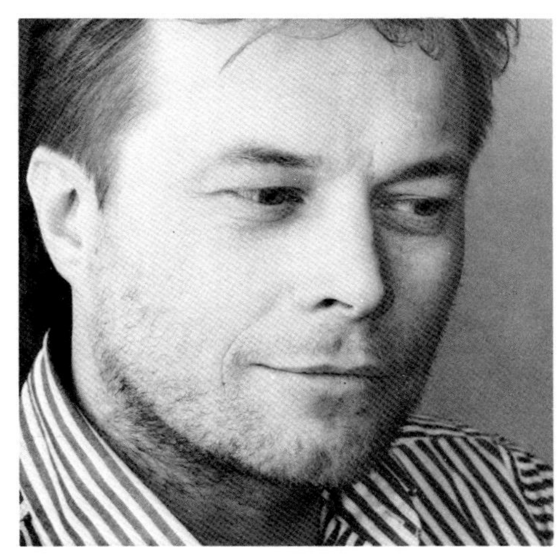

BIOGRAPHY

75

1950 Born, La Moure, North Dakota

1973 BFA, Metropolitan State College, Denver, Colorado

1976 MFA, University of California, Irvine

      Lives in Los Angeles

SOLO EXHIBITIONS

1980 Riko Mizuno Gallery, Los Angeles

1982 California State University, Los Angeles

1983 Riko Mizuno Gallery, Los Angeles

      Los Angeles Municipal Art Gallery, Los Angeles

      Installation Gallery, San Diego

      Sonoma State University, Sonoma, California

PUBLIC COMMISSIONS

1982 *Seattle Scatter*, Seattle Arts Commission, permanent sculptures at five sites, Seattle, Washington

1983 *Untitled Installation*, California Arts Council, commission for a permanent sculpture at Exposition Park, Los Angeles

1985 *Doorway Installation*, Community Redevelopment Agency, Los Angeles, California

SPECIAL PROJECTS

1983-84 Artist-Design Team Member, City of Phoenix Redevelopment Agency, Art in Public Places Program

1984-85 Artist Advisor Design Team Member, Santa Monica Redevelopment Project, Art in Public Places Program, Santa Monica, California

PUBLICATIONS

1980 *Dowser Fountain*, print edition, Cirrus Editions, Los Angeles

1978 *Heavenly Bodies*, self-published book

SELECTED GROUP EXHIBITIONS

1980 "Architectural Sculpture," Mount St. Mary's College, Fine Arts Gallery, Los Angeles

"Tableaux," Los Angeles Institute of Contemporary Art

1981 "Gallery Artists," Riko Mizuno Gallery, Los Angeles

"The Big Drawing Show," Newspace Gallery, Los Angeles

"Art in the Public Eye," Security Pacific Bank, Los Angeles

"Anti-Static," Baxter Art Gallery, California Institute of Technology, Pasadena

"Southern California Artists," Los Angeles Institute of Contemporary Art

1982 "Hang 8: Southern California Artists," Foundations Gallery, New York

"Sculpture '82," Sonoma State University, Sonoma, California

"Visiting Artists: 10 Years," Claremont Graduate School, Galleries East and West, Claremont, California

1983 "Sixteen Months at Art Center," Art Center College of Design, Pasadena

"The Nancy Yewell Collection," Baxter Art Gallery, California Institute of Technology, Pasadena

"Artists and the Theater," Herbert Palmer Gallery, Los Angeles

1984 "Aperto '84," 1984 Venice Biennale, Venice, Italy

"American Sculpture," Margo Leavin Gallery, Los Angeles

"Landescape," Marianne Deson Gallery, Chicago

BIBLIOGRAPHY

77

Bianchi, Tom, "Controlled Violence," *Artweek*, April 23, 1983, p. 7.

Blaine, Michael, "Architectural Spoof and Satire," *Artweek*, October 18, 1980, p. 20.

Burchett, Debra, "Visit: Kisch, Lere and Vogel," *Journal of the Los Angeles Institute of Contemporary Art*, October/November 1978.

Eals, Clay, "Scatterpiece," *West Seattle Herald*, August 8, 1984.

Hackett, Regina, *Seattle Times*, July 30, 1982.

Kelley, Jeff, "Installation in Conical Fantasy," *The San Diego Section*, November 25, 1983.

Knight, Christopher, "Breaking the Tyranny of the Automobile," *Los Angeles Herald Examiner*, August 26, 1984.

Komac, Dennis, "Spiralling Forces," *Artweek*, November 26, 1983, p. 4.

Lewis, Louise, "Experiences in Tableaux," *Artweek*, February 23, 1980, p. 5.

Montini, E.J., "Team Prepares Down-town Streetscape Design," *Arizona Republic*, December 13, 1983.

Muchnic, Suzanne, "Sculpture Becomes a Structure," *Los Angeles Times*, October 27, 1980.

Muchnic, Suzanne, "The Galleries," *Los Angeles Times*, November 21, 1980.

Pincus, Robert, "Portrait, Nature and Symbols on Exhibition at Barnsdall Park Gallery," *Los Angeles Times*, September 15, 1983.

Schwartz, Eric, "New Faces/New Images," *Ocular*, Spring 1981.

Spurrier, Jeff, "Olympic Spirits," *Los Angeles Reader*, June 1, 1984.

Stellweg, Carla, "Monument to Southern Hemisphere," *Artes Visuales*, Spring 1981.

Wilson, William, "Lere's 'Halo/Wheel,'" *Los Angeles Times*, September 4, 1984.

Wortz, Melinda, "Mathematical Whimsy," *Art News*, January 1981, pp. 73-77.

Wortz, Melinda, "Artists the Critics are Watching," *Art News*, May 1981, pp. 88-89.